Helen Edmundson

THE HERESY
OF LOVE

NICK HERN BOOKS
London
www.nickhernbooks.co.uk

HELEN EDMUNDSON

Helen Edmundson's first play, *Flying*, was presented at the
National Theatre Studio in 1990. In 1992, she adapted Tolstoy's
Anna Karenina for Shared Experience, for whom she also
adapted *The Mill on the Floss* in 1994. Both won awards – the
TMA and the Time Out Awards respectively – and both
productions were twice revived and extensively toured. Shared
Experience also staged her original adaptation of *War and Peace*
at the National Theatre in 1996, and toured her adaptations of
Mary Webb's *Gone to Earth* in 2004, Euripides' *Orestes* in 2006,
the new two-part version of *War and Peace* in 2008, and the
original play *Mary Shelley* in 2012. Her original play *The
Clearing* was first staged at the Bush Theatre in 1993, winning
the John Whiting and Time Out Awards, and *Mother Teresa is
Dead* was premiered at the Royal Court Theatre in 2002. Her
adaptation of Jamila Gavin's *Coram Boy* premiered at the
National Theatre to critical acclaim in 2005, receiving a Time
Out Award. It was subsequently revived in 2006, and produced
on Broadway in 2007. She adapted Calderón's *Life is a Dream*
for the Donmar Warehouse in 2009, and Arthur Ransome's
Swallows and Amazons for the Bristol Old Vic in 2010, which
subsequently transferred to the West End before embarking on a
national tour in 2012.

ABOUT THE ROYAL SHAKESPEARE COMPANY

The Royal Shakespeare Company at Stratford-upon-Avon was formed in 1960 and gained its Royal Charter in 1961. Last year we celebrated 50 years as a home for Shakespeare's work, the wider classical repertoire and new plays.

The founding Artistic Director, Peter Hall, created an ensemble theatre company of young actors and writers. The Company was led by Hall, Peter Brook and Michel Saint-Denis. The founding principles were threefold: the Company would embrace the freedom and power of Shakespeare's work, train and develop young actors and directors, and crucially, experiment in new ways of making theatre. There was a new spirit amongst this post-war generation and they intended to open up Shakespeare's plays as never before.

The impact of Peter Hall's vision cannot be underplayed. In 1955 he had premiered Samuel Beckett's *Waiting for Godot* in London, and the result was like opening a window during a storm.
The tumult of new ideas emerging across Europe in art, theatre and literature came flooding into British theatre. Hall channelled this new excitement into the setting up of the company in Stratford. Exciting breakthroughs took place in the rehearsal room and the studio day after day. The RSC became known for exhilarating performances of Shakespeare alongside new masterpieces such as *The Homecoming* and *Old Times* by Harold Pinter. It was a combination that thrilled audiences.

Peter Hall's rigour on classical text became legendary, but what is little known is that he applied everything he learned working on Beckett, and later on Harold Pinter, to his work on Shakespeare, and likewise he applied everything he learned from Shakespeare onto modern texts. This close and exacting relationship between writers from different eras became the fuel which powered the creativity of the RSC.

The search for new forms of writing and directing was led by Peter Brook. He pushed writers to experiment. "Just as Picasso set out to capture a larger slice of the truth by painting a face with several eyes and noses, Shakespeare, knowing that man is living his everyday life and at the same time is living intensely in the invisible world of his thoughts and feelings, developed a method through which we can see at one and the same time the look on a man's face and the vibrations of his brain."

A rich and varied range of writers flowed into the company and continue to do so. These include: Edward Albee, Howard Barker, Edward Bond, Howard Brenton, Marina Carr, Caryl Churchill, Martin Crimp, David Edgar, Peter Flannery, David Greig, Tony Harrison, Dennis Kelly, Tarell Alvin McCraney, Martin McDonagh, Rona Munro, Anthony Neilson, Harold Pinter, Stephen Poliakoff, Adriano Shaplin, Wole Soyinka, Tom Stoppard, debbie tucker green, Timberlake Wertenbaker and Roy Williams.

The RSC last year marked its 50th birthday with new productions of two of the Company's seminal plays: *The Homecoming* by Harold Pinter and *Marat/Sade* by Peter Weiss, adapted by Adrian Mitchell. Alongside these productions the Company welcomed back *Dunsinane* by David Greig and opened *Written on the Heart* by David Edgar in the Swan Theatre. New work this year includes plays by Helen Edmundson, James Fenton, Tamsin Oglesby and Adrian Mitchell. This year, Writer in Residence Mark Ravenhill will join the Company and will be working on two plays during his residency.

The RSC Ensemble is generously supported by THE GATSBY CHARITABLE FOUNDATION and THE KOVNER FOUNDATION

The RSC is grateful for the significant support of its principal funder, Arts Council England, without which our work would not be possible. Around 50 per cent of the RSC's income is self-generated from Box Office sales, sponsorship, donations, enterprise and partnerships with other organisations.

Supported by
ARTS COUNCIL ENGLAND

NEW WORK AT THE RSC

We are a contemporary theatre company built on classical rigour. We commission playwrights to engage with the muscularity and ambition of the classics. We have recently re-launched the RSC Studio to resource writers, directors and actors to explore and develop new ideas for our stages. We invite writers to spend time with us in our rehearsal rooms, with our actors and practitioners. Alongside developing their own plays for our stages, we invite them to contribute dramaturgically to both our main stage Shakespeare productions and our Young People's Shakespeares.

We believe that our writers help to establish a creative culture within the Company which both inspires new work and creates an ever more urgent sense of enquiry into the classics. The benefits work both ways. With our writers, our actors naturally learn the language of dramaturgical intervention and sharpen their interpretation of roles. Our writers benefit from re-discovering the stagecraft and theatre skills that have been lost over time. They regain the knack of writing roles for leading actors. They become hungry to use classical structures to power up their plays.

Mark Ravenhill is the Company's current Writer in Residence.

The RSC Literary Department is generously supported by THE DRUE HEINZ TRUST.

This production of *The Heresy of Love* was first performed by
the Royal Shakespeare Company in the Swan Theatre,
Stratford-upon-Avon, on 2 February 2012. The cast was as follows:

SISTER SEBASTIANA	**Teresa Banham**
FATHER ANTONIO	**Geoffrey Beevers**
ARCHBISHOP AGUIAR Y SEIJAS	**Stephen Boxer**
BISHOP SANTA CRUZ	**Raymond Coulthard**
JUANITA	**Dona Croll**
BRIGIDA	**Marty Cruickshank**
NUN	**Laura Darrall**
VICEREINE	**Catherine Hamilton**
MOTHER MARGUERITA	**Diana Kent**
PRIEST	**Youssef Kerkour**
JUANA INÉS DE LA CRUZ	**Catherine McCormack**
PRIEST	**Ian Midlane**
ANGELICA	**Sarah Ovens**
VICEROY	**Daniel Stewart**
DON HERNANDO	**Simon Thorp**

All other parts played by members of the Company.

Directed by	**Nancy Meckler**
Designed by	**Katrina Lindsay**
Lighting Designed by	**Ben Ormerod**
Music by	**Ilona Sekacz**
Sound Designed by	**John Leonard**
Movement by	**Liz Ranken**
Company Dramaturg	**Jeanie O'Hare**
Company Text and Voice work by	**Alison Bomber**
Dialect Coach	**Charmian Hoare**
Assistant Director	**Adam Lenson**
Musical Director	**Candida Caldicot**
Casting by	**Helena Palmer** cdg
Production Manager	**Rebecca Watts**
Costume Supervisor	**Sabine Lemaître**
Company Manager	**Jondon**
Stage Manager	**Suzanne Bourke**
Deputy Stage Manager	**Anna-Maria Casson**
Assistant Stage Manager	**Martha Mamo**

MUSICIANS

Soprano	**Anna Bolton**
Soprano	**Alexandra Saunders**
Mezzo-Soprano	**Hannah Rhodes**
Guitar	**Nicholas Lee**
Keyboard	**Candida Caldicot**
Percussion	**Kevin Waterman**

This text may differ slightly from the play as performed.

JOIN US

Join us from £18 a year.

Join today and make a difference
The Royal Shakespeare Company is an ensemble. We perform all year round in our Stratford-upon-Avon home, as well as having regular seasons in London, and touring extensively within the UK and overseas for international residencies.

With a range of options from £18 to £10,000 per year, there are many ways to engage with the RSC.

Choose a level that suits you and enjoy a closer connection with us whilst also supporting our work on stage.

Find us online
Sign up for regular email updates at **www.rsc.org.uk/signup**

Join today
Annual RSC Full Membership costs just £40 (or £18 for Associate Membership) and provides you with regular updates on RSC news, advance information and priority booking.

Support us
A charitable donation from £100 a year can offer you the benefits of membership, whilst also allowing you the opportunity to deepen your relationship with the Company through special events, backstage tours and exclusive ticket booking services.

The options include Shakespeare's Circle (from £100), Patrons' Circle (Silver: £1,000, Gold: £5,000) and Artists' Circle (£10,000).

For more information visit **www.rsc.org.uk/joinus** or call the RSC Membership Office on 01789 403 440.

THE ROYAL SHAKESPEARE COMPANY

Patron
Her Majesty the Queen

President
His Royal Highness The Prince of Wales

Artistic Director
Michael Boyd

Executive Director
Vikki Heywood

Board
Professor Jonathan Bate CBE
Michael Boyd (*Artistic Director*)
Damon Buffini
David Burbidge OBE
Miranda Curtis
Jane Drabble OBE
Noma Dumezweni
Mark Foster
Gilla Harris
Vikki Heywood (*Executive Director*)
John Hornby
Nigel Hugill (*Chairman*)
Baroness McIntosh of Hudnall
Paul Morrell OBE
Lady Sainsbury of Turville (*Deputy Chairman*)

The RSC was established in 1961. It is incorporated under Royal Charter
and is a registered charity, number 212481.

THE HERESY OF LOVE

Helen Edmundson

For Jonathan, Edwin and Eleanor

Author's Note

Sor (Sister) Juana Inés de la Cruz is a conundrum: a nun who wrote comic plays and secular poetry; a beautiful woman who shut herself away from the eyes of men; one of the greatest intellects of her time who ended by renouncing her right to a life of the mind. I first became fascinated by her in 2004, after seeing Nancy Meckler's vibrant production of her play *The House of Desires* at the Swan Theatre in Stratford-upon-Avon. I went away and read everything I could find about her, and to my relief discovered that, whilst certain facts are known about her and there are several extant documents relating to her life, there remain many unanswered questions about her motivations, beliefs and the state of her heart. Here, then, was room for invention. I decided early on that I wanted to try to write about her rather as a seventeenth-century Spanish playwright might have done. The context and high drama of her story seemed to invite this. So I have luxuriated in intrigues and rivalries, in disguised identities and mischievous servants. I have made full use of the bold and sudden contrast of the comic and the dramatic, characteristic of the period, and enjoyed forging a rhythmic and heightened language. I also decided to place her faith at the centre of the play, as this enabled me to explore some complex and challenging questions. What happens when we try to modify a belief system to suit the way in which we want to live? Must religions remain orthodox to remain potent and in order to survive? And why silence the women? Questions as relevant in our world, I think, as they were in Sister Juana's.

Helen Edmundson
January 2012

Characters

BISHOP SANTA CRUZ
FATHER ANTONIO
ARCHBISHOP AGUIAR Y SEIJAS
BRIGIDA
ANGELICA
JUANITA
SISTER SEBASTIANA
MOTHER MARGUERITA
SISTER JUANA
VICEROY
VICEREINE
DON HERNANDO

And NUNS, PRIESTS, MEMBERS OF THE COURT

This text went to press before the end of rehearsals and so may differ slightly from the play as performed.

ACT ONE

Scene One

The ARCHBISHOP's *palace, Mexico City. Evening.*

BISHOP SANTA CRUZ *is alone in a room, waiting.* FATHER
ANTONIO *enters.*

FATHER ANTONIO. Santa Cruz.

SANTA CRUZ. Good evening, Father Antonio. So you are
summoned too?

FATHER ANTONIO. Yes.

SANTA CRUZ. Do you know the cause? What matter is so
urgent that it cannot keep until tomorrow's council?

FATHER ANTONIO. I do not know. I was not told.

SANTA CRUZ. Yet not so urgent, it would seem, that we
should not be forced to wait like uninvited tradesmen.

I think our new Archbishop does not sleep.

You know him well, I understand – this Aguiar y Seijas.

FATHER ANTONIO. But there you are mistaken. Until I spoke
to him today before his consecration I had met him only
once: at Santiago de Compostela, at the university many
years ago. He began his studies as I finished mine. He
quickly gained a reputation for his fine, exacting mind, his
unremitting discipline.

SANTA CRUZ. I heard that he is zealous.

FATHER ANTONIO. Zealous, yes, on points of faith. And yet
it's said that if he's sometimes harsh with others he is a great
deal harsher with himself.

SANTA CRUZ. Some comfort then for Mexico.

FATHER ANTONIO. I hope you do not feel aggrieved, Santa
Cruz.

SANTA CRUZ. Aggrieved?

FATHER ANTONIO. As Bishop of Puebla you might have assumed that you would be the next Archbishop of Mexico.

SANTA CRUZ. I did not agitate for the position, nor did I expect it.

FATHER ANTONIO. Even so. The trust, the intimacy which you shared with our late Archbishop, were reason, I'm sure, for you to speculate.

SANTA CRUZ. I dared to hope, I'll grant you, yes, that my ten years' devoted service to this land, my standing amongst the people and my peers, might recommend me for advancement. But there. He did not elect himself. I would not presume to doubt our learned brothers in Madrid were guided solely by the Lord to the decision which they made.

FATHER ANTONIO. And you will stay on in Puebla now?

SANTA CRUZ. I will stay on in Puebla, yes. I will stay on in Puebla. Puebla is my diocese, my charge.

I am not governed by my pride.

ARCHBISHOP AGUIAR Y SEIJAS *enters*.

(*Standing and bowing*.) Your Grace.

ARCHBISHOP. Let us dispense with ceremony, the occasion does not warrant it.

SANTA CRUZ. Only allow me to extend, on behalf of the people of Puebla and myself, a heartfelt welcome to this great city of Mexico, and to this new and burgeoning land, so keenly desirous of your guidance and your love.

ARCHBISHOP. That this land is in need of guidance, I have no doubt, Santa Cruz. In your heartfelt welcome I find it harder to believe. I was born, you see, without imagination.

SANTA CRUZ. I do not speak what I do not mean.

ARCHBISHOP. No more do I.

I tried to see you earlier; I was told that you were otherwise engaged. You saw a play tonight, I understand, in the service of the Lord.

SANTA CRUZ. I saw a play at Court. It was written by a Sister
of the Church and performed in honour of your consecration.
I had thought to find you there and to pay you my respects
before the council in the morning.

ARCHBISHOP. I do not attend plays. I do not attend bullfights,
cockfights. I do not attend fiestas, or any other sordid
entertainment which the people feel the need to see played out
upon the streets. Nor do I expect to hear that my clergy do so.

SANTA CRUZ. It is not unusual in Mexico for a priest to attend
such an event. The complex and developing relationship
between the Court and ourselves, and all the diverse peoples,
has led to a system of concessions and demands which those
accustomed to the more solid ground of Spain do sometimes
find surprising.

ARCHBISHOP. You will not imply that my inexperience of this
country represents some disadvantage. It is my greatest
strength.

SANTA CRUZ. That was not my implication.

ARCHBISHOP. The reason, moreover, that I wear this ring and
you do not. You had better know this now. The 'concessions',
which you so openly acknowledge are cause for most acute
concern and anger in Madrid. Not one day have I been in this
city and already I have felt the consequences of my
predecessor's weakness for concession. My consecration, the
most solemn and profound of ceremonies, delayed and then
delayed because the Viceroy did not feel that it behove him to
arrive on time. Caravans of women traipsing into the
cathedral, their heads unveiled, laughing and chattering and
dressed as though to dance. At the west gate, I myself,
paraded, before I could prevent it, through some triumphal
archway, decorated all about with heathen and unholy words
which seemed to mock my office and to desecrate the very
House of God. Where is the Church? Where is the Church?
Tonight I stood alone in the highest room this palace could
afford and forced myself to gaze upon your darkening city. I
saw such scenes of dissolution and debauchery, replicated here
and there, in every square and street, so that I turned away and
bruised my eyes and wept to think the Lord should know what
I had seen.

SANTA CRUZ. I would urge you, then, to walk about this city in the sun: to see the several exquisite churches where even the most unruly of our people come willingly to pray; to visit our sacred convents with their gorgeous altars and their shady courtyards, our monasteries dispersed about the hills, astonishing in number. I would urge you to come to Puebla as my guest, to view the library I have established for the study of theology, the schools for virgin girls, the hospice I have founded there for the many indigent women who seek protection for their bodies and their souls.

ARCHBISHOP. Have no fear, Santa Cruz, I have been made aware of your special interest in the female sex.

SANTA CRUZ. I have long since grown oblivious to the base and scurrilous conjecture that such ministry attracts. I comfort myself with the thought that my spotless history and conduct might serve as some encouragement to those of my brothers similarly called. For it is vital work. The women enclosed in our cities are breathing proof of the civility of this society. The numbers of our women reserved in marriage to the Lord are unquestionable proof of the work which we have done. Many of our Criollo nuns have proved to be more pious and devoted than their Spanish sisters.

ARCHBISHOP. Devoted to what? To penning plays?

SANTA CRUZ. The nun who wrote the play is a particular case. There is not another like her, as far as I'm aware. For my part, I do not know her. However, my quiet friend, Father Antonio, has the honour of being her confessor.

FATHER ANTONIO. Yes, Your Grace. Sister Juana Inés de la Cruz, a Hieronymite nun in the Convent of San Jerónimo. She is indeed a particular case. She studies and writes prodigiously and has always done so. I knew her as a girl and encouraged her to profess in the hope that she might dedicate her gift to God. And for the most part, I would say…

ARCHBISHOP. But you are Censor for the Inquisition.

FATHER ANTONIO. Yes.

ARCHBISHOP. Then why do you not censor her?

FATHER ANTONIO. She has never thought or dared to write on matters of theology.

ARCHBISHOP. Or is the Inquisition another of our concessions?

FATHER ANTONIO. No, Your Grace. Much of her work is undertaken in honour of the Church. Simple hymns, carols and the like.

ARCHBISHOP. That is not her duty.

FATHER ANTONIO. It is complicated. Her pleasing personal qualities have led to her becoming a great favourite with the Court. The Vicereine, most especially, is her friend and benefactor.

ARCHBISHOP. Is she married to the Vicereine or to Christ?

FATHER ANTONIO. I must ask that you allow me to continue with my personal mission to set this woman on a righteous path. I will increase my efforts towards her reform.

ARCHBISHOP. We will not allow the Court to dictate to us in matters of obedience.

FATHER ANTONIO. The Viceroy is as King, Your Grace, and has the King's authority.

ARCHBISHOP. And what of that? We are not here to please the Court, to strike some hollow harmony, to look for favour nor for gratitude. We are not here to give the people what they think they want. We are here for their souls. For their immortal souls.

FATHER ANTONIO. And sometimes to secure their souls, as I'm sure you would agree, requires a little care, a moment's patience.

ARCHBISHOP. We must drag these people screaming and spitting, if need be, along the pathway to salvation. All else is vanity. Your vanity and self-gratification.

FATHER ANTONIO. Your Grace!

ARCHBISHOP. Harrowed in the torments and the fires of Hell, will they thank you then for your concessions? I think not.

Charity, yes, there must always be charity. Mercy, when it is truly called for, but we must never barter with our faith. And we must be exemplary. Let the people imitate our every word and deed. That is care. That is true care. If they wish to read, let them study their devotions. If they wish to write, let them set down their confessions. If they wish for spectacle, take them to the Auto da Fé and let them watch the changing lights of fallen men in flames.

Tomorrow I meet in council with my prelates. You know now what I am about. If you cannot stand with me, do not attend. Write to Madrid if you so desire. Request your immediate recall.

FATHER ANTONIO. There can be no question of that. How can you doubt... You must not doubt my loyalty.

SANTA CRUZ. Nor mine, Your Grace. I will not seek to humour you, I see at once it would not work, with quick assurances of my compliance, and I will sometimes burden you with questions and with caveats, but that should never make you doubt the depth of my respect. I see it is God's work you do. You have my trust and my support.

ARCHBISHOP (*to* FATHER ANTONIO). I want you to present to me the facts of every trial and case currently before the Inquisition.

FATHER ANTONIO. Now?

ARCHBISHOP. Yes. Now.

FATHER ANTONIO. There are certain papers I will need.

ARCHBISHOP. Then send for them.

FATHER ANTONIO *leaves to do so.*

I will see you at the council, Santa Cruz.

SANTA CRUZ. Yes, Your Grace.

ARCHBISHOP. Sleep well.

The ARCHBISHOP *leaves.*

SANTA CRUZ. Worse than I imagined then. This Aguiar y
Seijas. Twice the voting favoured me, they say. Twice I was
approved. The Lord alone knows what Jesuit contrivances
delivered him the final vote and heard his name proclaimed
upon the steps. Aguiar y Seijas. He wants me gone, of course
he does, will grasp at any pretext to send me traipsing down
the road to Veracruz with my boxes and my souvenirs of a
lifetime's ambition. Well, let him dream, if dream he can, for
he will not be rid of me. I was here before he came and will
be here when he is gone. A careful game is called for now. I
must meet his bluster with benignant sighs, his slanders with
humble politesse. I must speak only good of him abroad and
nobody must ever guess how I have lain awake at night and
ground each fraction of his name between my teeth. And all
the time I will torment him. With subtle craft and covert art,
I'll weave for him a shirt of hair more coarse, more chafing
and more sore than anything he ever felt against his testy
skin. He hates the Court. Then I'll start there, and with their
passion for the nun, that prodigy so prized by all. I'll send
him mad with scratching. And who can say, perhaps he'll
fall, demented, through the hidden cracks in this alert and
fitful ground. Mexico, it seems my loss is yours. Then let us
arm, and let us fight a quiet and most unholy war.

Scene Two

The locutory in the Convent of San Jerónimo.

*Wooden bars separate one side of the room from the other. At
one end of the bars there is a small entrance, which stands open.*

BRIGIDA *is making the room ready.* ANGELICA *enters from
within the convent.*

ANGELICA. Juanita! Brigida, where's Juanita?

BRIGIDA. Where she always is when there's work to be done:
nowhere to be seen. The useless slave.

ANGELICA. I need my clean veil.

BRIGIDA. They sent her to the market hours ago. She should be doing all this work, not me. It's her mistress they're coming here to see.

ANGELICA. What shall I do? I can't wear this one. Do you think she's in the kitchen?

BRIGIDA. A convent is no place for royalty. I'm sure there are plenty of servants at the palace to cook for the Viceroy and sing for the Viceroy. But no, they have to come here and put us to no end of trouble. And they'll arrive when they want to arrive and leave when they want to leave and make the sisters late for prayers.

ANGELICA. I'm glad they're coming.

BRIGIDA. I'm sure you are, señorita.

ANGELICA. How much can they see through the bars?

BRIGIDA. Too much. That's how much.

ANGELICA. Where do you think it might be?

BRIGIDA. What?

ANGELICA. My clean veil.

BRIGIDA. I don't know. And I wouldn't count on it being clean. That Juanita doesn't know where the laundry is. She ought to try having a mistress like mine, a mistress who knows how to mortify herself, then she'd learn what washing means.

JUANITA *enters from the convent.*

JUANITA. I just saw the funniest thing. I thought I'd die from laughing.

BRIGIDA. Where have you been?

ANGELICA. Juanita, I need my clean veil.

JUANITA. There was one of those illusas in the marketplace.

BRIGIDA. I don't want to hear it. Help me with this.

JUANITA. An Indian woman. About my age.

ANGELICA. What's an illusas?

JUANITA. A woman who says she has visions. Visions of the Lord.

BRIGIDA. As though the Lord would reveal Himself to an Indian.

JUANITA. She said she was looking for fifteen people who were ready to exchange their hearts with Jesus Christ.

BRIGIDA. What blasphemy.

JUANITA. She had this big crowd around her. And she said the Lord had asked her to find these fifteen people. And all these men and women are standing round and some of them are really thinking about whether to do the swapping hearts. All serious and worrying.

BRIGIDA. Out of my way. You tell more tales than your mistress.

JUANITA. And then she falls down on the ground and goes into a sort of trance. And her eyes roll back in her head and she starts making these sighing sounds – 'oh, ah, ohh, ah, ah, ah, ah' – and she says the Lord has come upon her and she's panting and groaning faster and faster. And all the people are staring at her and whispering about a state of ecstasy, and I'm thinking I recognise that state of ecstasy and it wasn't the Lord who took me there.

BRIGIDA. Don't be disgusting.

ANGELICA. What do you mean?

JUANITA. Oh, Brigida, so you know what I'm talking about.

BRIGIDA. The woman's mad. She should be locked away.

JUANITA. Someone said she's married to a tailor who lives behind the cathedral. I'd like to hear their conversation at dinner time. 'What did you do today, dear?' 'Oh, I sewed two shirts and a fine leather jerkin. What did you do?' 'Oh, I got down on all fours in the marketplace and suckled the Christ Child.'

BRIGIDA. You be quiet!

JUANITA. As God is my witness, that's what she said she was doing. Only there was no Christ Child there. Just this great big bosom dripping milk and all the men pushing forward to get a closer look.

BRIGIDA. Disgusting. Disgusting talk.

ANGELICA. Did she have a baby?

JUANITA. And then this priest comes hurrying through the crowd. And you should have seen his face. And he takes off his cloak and tries to cover her up, but she struggles and ducks and runs off down an alleyway.

BRIGIDA. She won't be so brazen once the Inquisition get hold of her.

JUANITA. What harm is she doing? If she was a nun and saying all that, they'd have carried her off to the Pope by now and made a saint of her.

BRIGIDA. You stop that heathen talk.

JUANITA. I'm no more heathen than you are.

SISTER SEBASTIANA *enters from the direction of the convent gate*.

SEBASTIANA. They're here. Is everything ready?

BRIGIDA. Yes, mistress. I've done the best I can.

SEBASTIANA (*to* ANGELICA). What are you doing out here?

ANGELICA. Sorry, sister.

JUANITA. She was helping me.

SEBASTIANA. Go and tell the sisters that the Viceroyals are arriving. And tell Mother Prioress that the Bishop of Puebla is with them.

BRIGIDA. The Bishop of Puebla?

SEBASTIANA (*to* ANGELICA). Go.

ANGELICA. Yes, sister. (*Hesitating*.) My clean veil, Juanita?

JUANITA. On the end of your bed, where it's supposed to be.

ANGELICA *runs into the convent*.

SEBASTIANA. Close the gate behind me, Brigida.

BRIGIDA. Yes, mistress.

SISTER SEBASTIANA *passes through the gate in the bars.*
BRIGIDA *shuts the gate.*

On the convent side of the bars, the NUNS *enter, singing.*
MOTHER MARGUERITA, SISTER SEBASTIANA *and*
SISTER JUANA *are amongst them.*

On the gate side, the VICEROYAL COUPLE *enter,*
accompanied by members of the Court, including DON
HERNANDO, *and by* BISHOP SANTA CRUZ. *They listen*
with pleasure to the SISTERS' *music. As it finishes there is a*
silence, as all wait for the VICEROY *to speak.*

VICEROY. Sisters, my silence is a tribute to the beauty of your
voices. Forgive me, Mother Prioress. I am all gratitude.
There is no balm more soothing, nor diverting it appears, for
my overburdened mind.

MOTHER MARGUERITA. Thank you, Your Excellency.
Though watchful of inciting pride, we have ever felt, in
praising God, the urge to strive towards perfection.

VICEREINE. Perfection indeed. And proof, if proof should be
required, that through your great devotion and your prayers
you are imbued with something of the angels, and occupy a
sacred realm halfway, I think, between this Earth and Heaven.

MOTHER MARGUERITA. You honour us, Your Excellency.
We value beyond expression your kindness and your
constancy.

And I must turn to you, Bishop Santa Cruz, and bid you
heartfelt welcome to our convent home. We are
overwhelmed with joy to find you here amongst us. How
often have we wished this day would come.

SANTA CRUZ. The excellent sisters of San Jerónimo – it is a
phrase I have heard too many times to number. Only my
work in Puebla has kept me from your door.

MOTHER MARGUERITA. Then we are happily neglected. We
marvel at each fresh report of your endeavours.

SANTA CRUZ. And there is one specific cause, I will admit, induced me to accompany Don Tomas here today. For last night, as his guest, I saw a play performed at Court, written, as I understand, by one who lives amongst you.

VICEROY. Yes. Where is Sister Juana? Let Sister Juana come closer to the grille, for we would speak some words to her.

SISTER JUANA *approaches the bars.*

SANTA CRUZ. Sister Juana Inés de la Cruz.

JUANA. My lord.

SANTA CRUZ. You are not as I imagined you would be.

JUANA. Might I ask in what way, my lord?

SANTA CRUZ. You write beyond your years, as well as beyond your habit.

JUANA. I am not as young as I appear. As for this habit which I wear, it is, I find, as Perseus' helm of darkness: the secret of invisibility, my pass to all the world.

SANTA CRUZ. I thought your play exceptional.

JUANA. Thank you, my lord.

SANTA CRUZ. I thought it witty. I thought it intriguing. And intelligent in the extreme. Had someone told me it was penned by one of the celebrated dramatists of Spain, I would not have questioned it. It compared most favourably.

JUANA. You do me too much honour.

SANTA CRUZ. Nor did I find it lacking in morality. There was a rightness in it from the start which pleased me greatly.

VICEREINE. It was a triumph, Sister Juana, as I always knew it would be. The Court was never so enchanted nor so united in its praise. Is that not so, Don Tomas?

VICEROY. Indeed. Mexico is fortunate to count such talent as its own.

JUANA. It is a play. A little play, I claim no greatness for it. Yet it was written at Your Excellencies' behest, to mark a most auspicious day, and so for that I worked it with my heart, and so for that I am relieved and gratified to know that it was happily received.

MOTHER MARGUERITA. And our new Archbishop? I hope it pleased him too?

VICEREINE. The Archbishop was not able to attend.

JUANA. He was not there?

MOTHER MARGUERITA. That is a pity.

VICEROY. Though I had made it plain to him the evening was in his honour.

SANTA CRUZ. I'm sure he would not stay away without good cause.

MOTHER MARGUERITA. Of course. He is still recovering, perhaps, from the rigours of his voyage.

VICEREINE. Sister Juana, please accept this token of our gratitude and our esteem.

A box is passed to SISTER JUANA *through the bars. She opens it. It contains a gold necklace.*

JUANA. How beautiful. Your Excellencies, I am humbled by your generosity.

VICEREINE. As we are ever humbled by your gifts.

JUANA. Sisters, look, for this is yours as much as mine, and you must claim some credit. Each time you let me be excused my duties in the sewing room, or stilled your hands when you had thought to knock upon my door, was worth another line to me.

VICEREINE. Then, good sisters, we applaud you too.

JUANA. And there were many times when, in the common room at night, I forced my sisters to read out the scenes I'd worked upon that day, so I could understand the music which the different voices made and so refine the verse.

MOTHER MARGUERITA. It was a great amusement to us all. We needed little coaxing.

JUANA. Mother Marguerita I commandeered to play the stern and righteous father, for as you see, we want for men and could not cast to type.

VICEREINE. I wish I could have seen this strange rehearsal.

JUANA. And even our imposing Sister of the Gate, Sister Sebastiana, relented and agreed to read the scheming Doña Ana, quite against her nature I might add.

SEBASTIANA. I saw no harm in it, my lord. For it was in our leisure hour and gave us much to contemplate.

SANTA CRUZ. I see no harm in it at all. It was a service to your sister and thereby to the Court.

DON HERNANDO. And what of your heroine, Sister Juana? I venture to suppose that it was you who read the part. For those of us who knew you when you first arrived at Court, agreed that in that glorious and too desired girl, you merely wrote a study of yourself.

JUANA. Wily Don Hernando, I will admit that there is something of myself in Leonor, and yet I called upon my niece to read the part. Come here, my sweet Angelica.

ANGELICA *comes to stand beside* SISTER JUANA.

Your Excellencies, my lord, may I present my beloved niece Angelica, my brother's child, who has lately come to live within our walls.

VICEREINE. Angelica. A pretty name. You must be proud of your aunt, and all that she's accomplished.

ANGELICA. I am, Your Majesty. Your Excellency. I read her play a hundred times, and learned my speeches off by heart. I helped her to make copies too, though my hand is not as neat or clear as it should be. I'm told.

VICEROY. And do you mean to profess, child?

ANGELICA. Perhaps. I am not certain.

JUANA. It is my brother's dearest wish, though he does not insist upon it.

MOTHER MARGUERITA. We hope to guide Angelica towards her calling.

DON HERNANDO. I'll wager that she's taken vows before the year is out. For, as I've learned to my regret, all our loveliest maidens do.

SANTA CRUZ. Think carefully, señorita, before you turn your back on such an opportunity. There are countless women who would gladly take your place.

ANGELICA. I will, my lord.

SANTA CRUZ. Sister Juana, may I speak with you?

JUANA. Of course.

MOTHER MARGUERITA. Pass beyond the grille, my lord.

The gate is opened and SANTA CRUZ *passes through.*

VICEREINE. And with your permission, Mother Prioress, we will sit a while and partake of these delights you have so lovingly prepared.

MOTHER MARGUERITA. Servants, attend their Excellencies.

The SISTERS *withdraw from* SISTER JUANA *and* SANTA CRUZ.

SANTA CRUZ. I will be brief, for I must soon return to Puebla.

JUANA. I'm sorry. I had hoped that you would come and see my library. I have heard so much of yours. Though mine, I'm sure, is modest by comparison, I think there are some volumes there would interest you.

SANTA CRUZ. Someone told me that a book is never printed in Spain without a copy being sent to you.

JUANA. An exaggeration, I'm afraid – I am surrounded by them. Although I am most fortunate in the books which I receive.

SANTA CRUZ. I will explore it next time, if I may.

JUANA. I would be honoured.

SANTA CRUZ. Sister Juana, Archbishop Aguiar y Seijas does not share my admiration for your work.

JUANA. Does he not? How troubling. I wonder what he can have read. Perhaps an early sonnet. Some of them were clumsy, I admit.

SANTA CRUZ. It is not the quality of your work, as I suspect you know, which he objects to. But rather that it is your work.

JUANA. Because I am a woman? Or because I am a nun?

SANTA CRUZ. I question whether he recognises the existence of women beyond the Church. But as for those within it, he holds admirably strong and rigid views on what constitutes their duty.

JUANA. This is not the first time I have encountered this kind of opposition.

SANTA CRUZ. From an Archbishop?

JUANA. No. Not from an Archbishop. But when I decided to profess, I spent many hours, days, in discussion and in prayer with His Reverence, Father Antonio Núñez de Miranda, my Father Confessor. I came to feel quite certain, as I still feel now, that I can reconcile my writing and my studies with my vocation. I am sure that Father Antonio will speak to the Archbishop on my behalf, and reassure him that I am in no way neglectful of my duty.

SANTA CRUZ. Father Antonio was there with me when the Archbishop made his feelings clear. He spoke not a word on your behalf. I would rather say that he was pleased to find an ally willing to condemn you.

SISTER JUANA *is visibly shocked.*

JUANA. I see.

SANTA CRUZ. I tell you this in confidence.

JUANA. I understand.

SANTA CRUZ. The Archbishop is an extraordinary man. Whilst I would not advocate opposing him in anything, I hope you now at least have time to search your heart and stand prepared.

JUANA. Thank you.

SANTA CRUZ. At this morning's council, he announced reforms which will affect us all. Gatherings in the locutories, such as this, visits to sisters from friends and family will soon become impossible.

JUANA. He cannot stop their Excellencies from coming here.

SANTA CRUZ. He will try.

I will come and speak with you again next time I'm in the city.

JUANA. Thank you. Yes.

The inscription which I wrote for the triumphal archway; was he not made aware of that?

SANTA CRUZ. He was. He disliked its classical themes, and what he termed its allusion to ancient Mexico.

JUANA. Does he mean to deny that Mexico existed before the Spanish came? Mexico and women; I think his time here will be difficult.

SANTA CRUZ. We must hope that it is not.

JUANA. Yes. Forgive me. I sometimes have a tendency to be too strident in my expression. It is a trait I labour to control.

SANTA CRUZ. Something else we have in common.

Think of me as a friend, Sister Juana.

JUANA. I will. I do, my lord.

BISHOP SANTA CRUZ *leaves*. SISTER JUANA *goes to join the* SISTERS, *who are singing*.

Scene Three

SISTER JUANA*'s cell.* JUANITA *enters with the box containing the new gold necklace, and places it on* SISTER JUANA*'s desk. She leaves.*

ANGELICA *enters and sees the box. She goes to it and opens it and takes out the necklace.*

JUANITA *enters.*

JUANITA. Señorita Angelica! You put that down right now.

ANGELICA *does so, and moves away.*

ANGELICA. Sorry, Juanita. I was just…

JUANITA. No one is allowed to touch Sister Juana's things. Except me.

She goes to the desk and takes the necklace out of the box.

Well, come here then.

ANGELICA *laughs and goes to her.* JUANITA *fastens the necklace around her neck, and holds up a mirror for her.*

ANGELICA. Look. I am transformed. No more a country girl. I am a woman. I am a lady of the Court. And Don Hernando is my lover.

JUANITA. Don Hernando!

ANGELICA. He said I was lovely.

JUANITA. He was talking about Sister Juana. You don't understand the way these courtiers speak. They look at you and move their mouths, but the words are meant for someone else.

ANGELICA. He smiled at me. Through the bars.

JUANITA. For him it has always been Sister Juana. You should have seen him when we lived at Court. She was very young then. Not much older than you are now. He was following her everywhere, offering her trinkets, trapping her in corners, falling about like he had no bones in him.

ANGELICA. Did she succumb?

JUANITA. Where do you get your words from? No, she did not 'succumb'. She had her mind on other things. Now the closest he can get is paying her to write him poems to send to other women.

ANGELICA. What sort of poems?

JUANITA. Oh, poems telling them they're beautiful. Poems telling them he needs them. And poems telling them to go away.

ANGELICA. He's very handsome.

JUANITA. Ha. The man's three times as old as you. Strip away those fancy clothes and you might get a nasty shock. That's all I'm saying.

ANGELICA. What do you mean?

JUANITA. That Bishop Santa Cruz, now he's another case entirely. There is a man most surely formed in God's own image. He could make me confess to anything.

Footsteps and voices are heard approaching.

ANGELICA. She's coming!

JUANITA. Take it off. Take it off.

She takes the necklace from ANGELICA *and replaces it in the box.*

Away, away, away.

ANGELICA *rushes off to her room.*

SISTER JUANA *and the* VICEREINE *enter.*

VICEREINE. It was astonishing. Truly astonishing.

JUANA. Thank you, Juanita, you may leave us.

JUANITA *leaves.*

VICEREINE. It seemed so effortless. So accomplished. As though you had written a hundred plays before.

JUANA. But did people laugh? No one has told me that yet. For most of all it is a comedy. And laughter is the hardest thing to speculate upon.

VICEREINE. They laughed at everything. Except when they were not supposed to.

JUANA. At what most especially?

VICEREINE. Most especially at the servingman, I would say.

JUANA. That's good. That's very good. And the actress playing Leonor, I hope she did not simper?

VICEREINE. Not at all. She was strong and understood the wit. She was very like you. I was so proud of you, Juana. And all the time I wished that you were sitting there beside me.

It seemed so wrong that you should not be there.

JUANA. I would not have wanted that at all. To sit beside you, yes. Yes. But not to see the play. A mother should not sit and watch beside her daughter's nuptial bed.

VICEREINE. How extraordinary you are.

What did you think of Bishop Santa Cruz?

JUANA. He is all I hoped he would be. We have heard great things about his work.

VICEREINE. He is an excellent man. He is a man to trust. A cleric who can look a woman in the eye, and they are rare indeed. I have said to him what I will say to you, Juana: that when this new Archbishop finally deigns to come before me, I will leave him in no doubt of your unrivalled status, both in this land and in my heart.

JUANA. You are too kind.

VICEREINE. You are an example to the world. He should be thanking you, beatifying you – a second saint for Mexico, instead of meeting you with censure and with disrespect.

JUANA. I'm sure that he will soon discover subjects more deserving of his wrath and he will leave me be.

VICEREINE. If he does not, he will be chastened thoroughly.
I'll write a letter to Madrid and he'll be made to comprehend
the power of my name and line.

JUANA. Poor man, I almost pity him. He has just arrived, that's
all. He wants to make his mark.

VICEREINE. Then let him make it elsewhere. I will not let him
touch you. And as for this notion that I should not be allowed
to visit you...

JUANA. Now, that I think we have to stop.

VICEREINE. The Lord knows there are weeks, days, when I
only live to come here. To talk to you. My one true friend.

JUANA. Maria.

The VICEREINE *seems suddenly emotional.*

I hope there is nothing troubling you. Maria?

VICEREINE. There is another baby. I think there is another
baby.

JUANA. You are with child?

VICEREINE. It will die, of course, like all the rest, before it's
even born.

JUANA. No. You cannot know that.

VICEREINE. It will. There is no point in hoping it will not.
Hope has been my greatest enemy.

It is a sort of punishment. Though I cannot think for what. It
must have been a grave offence that I should be so mortified.

JUANA. God is not punishing you. Why would he? It is life and
death. Only that.

Have you told Don Tomas?

VICEREINE. No. I cannot bear to see the look of panic in his
eyes. Another thing for him to fear. Sometimes I think he
cannot blink without advisers to instruct him.

JUANA. But you must tell him. And send for your physician, as
soon as you get back.

VICEREINE. I thought it would have disappeared by now. This one is more inclined than most to cling onto the walls of me. This one will stay a while, I think. Long enough to kick perhaps. To flutter. Long enough to make me crave it in my arms. Then one day it will decide it's time. And it will twist and wrench and slip away from me into a waiting pail.

JUANA. My darling. My darling. If I could take all your pain upon myself I would. I truly would.

And I will pray for you, and for your child.

VICEREINE. I would rather have your prayers than anyone's. I think God listens to your prayers.

I must go. We're holding a reception for the Peruvian Ambassador tonight, and it will be hours of work to make me ready.

I'm sorry, Juana.

JUANA. What for?

VICEREINE. This is your day. A day to celebrate how wondrous you are. But I wanted you to know. I may be absent suddenly within the coming weeks. Now you will know why.

I think I must walk out alone, for I might cry to leave you.

JUANA. Juanita!

They embrace.

VICEREINE. What if the sin is his? I do not think he has the strength to give to me a living child.

JUANITA enters.

JUANITA. Yes, mistress?

JUANA. The Vicereine has to leave now.

VICEREINE. Goodbye, Sister Juana.

JUANA. I will write to you.

The VICEREINE *nods, and leaves with* JUANITA.

After a moment, SISTER JUANA *goes to her desk and picks up the necklace carefully. She removes the large cross she is wearing around her neck and holds the necklace in its place.*

SISTER SEBASTIANA *enters, unseen by* SISTER JUANA, *and watches her for a moment.*

SEBASTIANA. It looks well on you.

JUANA. Sebastiana. Yes. It is a generous gift and more than I deserve.

SEBASTIANA. Father Antonio is here to speak with you.

JUANA. I am not expecting him.

SEBASTIANA. Will you see him in the chapel or in here?

JUANA. I will see him in here. Thank you.

SEBASTIANA. You are welcome.

SISTER SEBASTIANA *leaves.* SISTER JUANA *returns the necklace to its case.*

FATHER ANTONIO *enters.*

FATHER ANTONIO. Sister Juana.

JUANA. Your Reverence.

FATHER ANTONIO. I trust that you are well.

JUANA. Quite well, thank you. I was not aware that I am due confession.

FATHER ANTONIO. You are not.

Sister Juana, I thought I saw the Vicereine just now, passing through the courtyard.

JUANA. Yes. She has just left me.

FATHER ANTONIO. You received her in your cell?

JUANA. Yes. I sometimes do. I thought you knew that.

FATHER ANTONIO. I did not. And I must ask that you refrain from doing so again.

JUANA. So if she were to ask to speak to me in private, or to view my library shelves that she might choose a book to read, you would have me tell her no.

FATHER ANTONIO. Yes. I would have you tell her no.

JUANA. Very well. If you can tell me why I should.

FATHER ANTONIO. Because it is against the rules. It is against the rules for anyone, excepting members of this community, or clergy like myself, to pass into the cloister, as you are well aware.

JUANA. The Vicereine, surely, is a special case.

FATHER ANTONIO. The rule applies to everyone.

JUANA. Nor can I see the harm in it. Mother Marguerita has never felt it necessary to withhold permission.

FATHER ANTONIO. Then I shall speak to Mother Marguerita before I leave. You may receive the Vicereine in the locutory. That is what it's there for. That the bars are sometimes drawn aside is enough, I am quite certain, to allow for any necessary contact.

JUANA. May I send for some refreshment, Father? You seem a little hot.

FATHER ANTONIO. No. I do not need refreshment. And I must also insist that you decline should you be approached by the Court, or by anyone, to write another play.

JUANA. Again, may I ask why?

FATHER ANTONIO. There is a feeling, a consensus, that it is not seemly for a sister of the Church to write on matters secular.

JUANA. My play was a great success, I understand, and reflected favourably upon this order and the Church.

FATHER ANTONIO. And it has come to my attention that you are writing poems, commissions from members of the Court. Poems which speak of love and so forth, relations between male and female. That must also stop.

JUANA. I fear that even you cannot put an end to 'love and so forth'.

FATHER ANTONIO. The poems must stop, is what I mean.

JUANA. You are condemning me to poverty. I need the money I am paid for the writing work I undertake. You know more than anyone that unlike many of my sisters I have no fortune of my own. Would you have me dismiss my servants? My slave? Clean my own cell, prepare my own meals?

FATHER ANTONIO. I'm sure you could find another means of income. There are people you could apply to.

JUANA. But I do not need to. The poems, like the play, are harmless. They are a favour and a service to those who ask for them. Nothing more. You know that I do not seek glory. You know I value this facility which some would say I have with words only in so much that it is given me by God. And you have agreed with me, no, you have counselled me, that it would be ingratitude, a form of arrogance on my behalf were I to waste this gift.

FATHER ANTONIO. I may have said that in the past.

JUANA. You brought to me, not many months ago, a delegation from the Cathedral Chapter, who asked me to compose some verses to decorate their ceremonial arch. And three times I refused because I feared I was unworthy of the honour, and three times you returned with them. And you spoke to Mother Prioress so that she intervened on their behalf, and I could do nothing but concede.

FATHER ANTONIO. That was different. That was a service to the Church.

JUANA. An allegory. On classical lines. That is what they asked for and that is what they got. A poem, Father.

I entered this convent, this order on your recommendation, because it is not so austere as some. Because it would allow me to continue with my studies and my work. You knew that and you accepted that.

FATHER ANTONIO. No. No. No. I knew it, yes, but it was always my hope that with my continued guidance and the love and example of your sisters, you would cease in time to feel the need of intellectual pursuit. And I have spoken with the new Archbishop, and he has revealed to me the depth of the disquiet this matter causes me.

JUANA. Ah. So this is the new Archbishop.

FATHER ANTONIO. No.

JUANA. You are speaking for the Archbishop.

FATHER ANTONIO. I am speaking for myself. I am at fault. I do not deny that. I have been too lenient, too easily distracted, and I will search my conscience, and where I have been at fault I will do penance for it. I feel, I strongly suspect, that you are using Mother Church, Sister Juana, and you must not use the Church. You are setting yourself up above all right authority.

JUANA. I set myself up above no one.

FATHER ANTONIO. The meaning and purpose of your life now lies in prayer. In prayer and nothing else.

JUANA. Are you questioning my faith?

FATHER ANTONIO. I know beneath it all your faith is sound.

JUANA. I am at prayer as often as my sisters. And frequently I pray alone.

FATHER ANTONIO. I do not doubt that.

JUANA. Or am I singled out somehow? Expected to be more pious, more devout than any other living soul?

FATHER ANTONIO. No.

JUANA. I have a talent so I must be punished for it. There were brothers, priests in Spain whose plays were widely lauded. Were they subject to such special scrutiny, required to be so preternaturally perfect in their devotion?

FATHER ANTONIO. That is different. Times were different then.

JUANA. Yes, of course, it was different for them.

FATHER ANTONIO. You renounced the world, Sister Juana.

JUANA. But I did not renounce my mind!

Your Reverence... I mean no disrespect.

FATHER ANTONIO. Juana. Child. You know my one concern is for the welfare of your soul.

JUANA. Is it? Still? Because if it is not, if you have suddenly developed such grave misgivings in regard to me, then perhaps it would be better if I place my soul in other hands.

FATHER ANTONIO. Absolutely not. You are too hasty.

JUANA. If you cannot find it in your conscience to support me.

FATHER ANTONIO. I cannot always say what you would have me say. My counsel will not always be what you would want to hear. That is not my duty. Nor should you wish that it were so, for what then would that say about your pride?

The morning you at last professed, I myself, with trembling hands, lit the candles on the altar. When you spoke your vows I wept for joy and gratitude.

JUANA. I know.

FATHER ANTONIO. What cause have you to doubt me?

I am advising you, asking you, to set aside your pen and write no more.

JUANA. But I cannot do that. I tried it once before, do you remember? My pen, my ink, papers, books, all were locked away from me and yet I did not cease to write; composing verses in my head, memorising them, studying the nature of the things around me, speculating, theorising. It is what I do. It is what I am. I do it even in my sleep.

'He has made many keys to Heaven, and there are many mansions for people of as many different natures.' How often have you said that to me? I have not changed.

FATHER ANTONIO. We must not allow this to become a crisis. We must not.

JUANA. I do not look for any crisis.

FATHER ANTONIO. For your own sake, Sister Juana, spend some time in silent contemplation. Consider all that I have said. Open your soul and pray to God. Heed His wisdom if you will not heed mine.

I will see you at confession.

Sister Juana?

JUANA. Yes. Yes. Thank you, Your Reverence.

FATHER ANTONIO. And you will pray?

JUANA. Yes. You may tell His Grace that I will pray.

FATHER ANTONIO *looks at her for a moment, and then leaves.*

Scene Four

In the locutory. SISTER SEBASTIANA *is escorting* FATHER ANTONIO *out.*

SEBASTIANA. Your Reverence, may I speak to you?

FATHER ANTONIO. You may.

SEBASTIANA. It is about Sister Juana.

FATHER ANTONIO. What of Sister Juana? Tell me.

SEBASTIANA. I want to say, that should someone be minded to attempt to put an end to her unorthodox activities, or to subject her way of life to closer scrutiny, that person would not be without support. I do not believe I am the only sister who is unsettled, both physically and spiritually, by her conduct, and the disturbance which it brings into our home.

FATHER ANTONIO. Why do you say this to me now?

SEBASTIANA. I sense there is a growing feeling of unease regarding her.

FATHER ANTONIO. I am glad that you have told me this.
Because I would not wish you to repeat what you have said
to anyone. You had not arrived in Mexico, perhaps, when the
Carmelite Convent of San José was put on trial for heresy.
Factions are a dangerous thing, and they can lead to more
calamity than you have wit to contemplate.

SEBASTIANA. I only meant…

FATHER ANTONIO. Sister Juana may be a rare and complex
creature, but she is no less devout than you or I. Look to
yourself before you dare to judge her.

I bid you goodnight.

Scene Five

In SISTER JUANA'*s cell. Late evening. In the chapel, some of
the nuns are practising their singing, and their voices drift in on
the air.* SISTER JUANA *is standing at the window, gazing out.
She is troubled.* ANGELICA *enters.*

ANGELICA. I've come to say goodnight.

JUANA. Goodnight, my little one. Have you enjoyed your day?

ANGELICA. Oh, yes. So much.

JUANA. Did you think the Vicereine beautiful?

ANGELICA. Oh, yes. Though not as beautiful as you. Juana, is
it true that when you lived at Court, all the men were in love
with you?

JUANA. Of course it isn't. Another exaggeration.

ANGELICA. But some of them were. Juanita said so.

JUANA. Did she?

ANGELICA. How did you look when you were at Court? What
colour dresses did you wear?

JUANA. I can't remember. It's so very long ago.

ANGELICA. But you must remember. How did you wear your hair?

JUANA. I don't know.

I had one dress…

ANGELICA. Yes?

JUANA. It was velvet. Pale-blue velvet with gold embroidery. And lace around the bodice.

ANGELICA. Where is it now?

JUANA. Oh, I gave away all my dresses when I came here.

ANGELICA. How could you bear to?

JUANA. It wasn't hard. It was a relief in a way.

ANGELICA. You should have kept it for me.

JUANA. How could I know that you would come along?

Off to bed now. There are only hours till matins.

ANGELICA. Why did you have to come here?

JUANA. I wanted to come here. I knew this was where I should be.

ANGELICA. Is that the same as a 'calling'?

JUANA. Angelica, if someone tells you that one night you will awaken and hear God's voice telling you to become a Sister of the Church, you mustn't believe them. You must listen to your heart.

Go to bed now.

ANGELICA *hugs her.*

ANGELICA. Can I have a new dress?

JUANA. We'll see.

ANGELICA *runs off.* SISTER JUANA*'s gaze returns to the window. After a few moments* JUANITA *enters.*

JUANITA. That girl is so excited. I don't think she's found her calling yet.

Shall I light the candles in your chamber?

JUANITA *crosses to the window.*

Oh... Now, that is a moon to wonder at.

JUANA. Look how clear, how close the valley seems. God's lantern. I fancied I could see the village. I fancied if I stood here long enough I might see Mother in the fields, rounding up the horses for the night.

JUANITA. Are you wishing you were back there?

JUANA. No. Though sometimes I can't help thinking how simple, how peaceful everything would be if I could be satisfied by growing fruit and rearing lambs.

Pause.

JUANITA. You seem a little sad tonight. What's happened?

JUANA. Do you remember when we rowed out on the lake that night, Juanita? It was our Saint's day, and Mother let us take the boat. We rowed until we could see nothing but the water and the sky. And the moon, the moon was just as it is now; pregnant, and sublime. And we lay inside the boat and closed our eyes, and rocked. And there was only us. And God was holding us. God was the water and the sky and our breath. Do you remember?

JUANITA. I remember that my arms were aching for a week from all that rowing.

JUANA. Do you remember? You were singing.

JUANITA. Yes. I remember. Of course I remember.

JUANA. I've never been so happy as I was at that moment. So complete.

Pause.

JUANITA. Come now. I think you should go to bed. You're tired, and after such a day of glory as it's been. I'll light the candles.

JUANA. No. No, you go, Juanita. I have to write.

JUANITA *leaves.* SISTER JUANA *goes to her desk and sits down. She picks up her pen and writes.*

ACT TWO

Scene One

In the locutory. The bars have been drawn aside. SISTER
JUANA, MOTHER MARGUERITA, ANGELICA *and*
SISTER SEBASTIANA *are sitting with the* VICEREINE, DON
HERNANDO *and* BISHOP SANTA CRUZ. *The* VICEREINE
is now visibly pregnant. JUANITA *and* BRIGIDA *are in
attendance.*

DON HERNANDO. It was unspeakable. The Archbishop is a
kind of alchemist; I swear he turned a single hour into
eternity.

VICEREINE. The cathedral was stifling. One of my women
fainted.

DON HERNANDO. The first part of his sermon was a dry and
convoluted treatise on the manifestations of Christ's love for
Man. At least, I think that's what it was. I followed not the
half of it. Theology for theologians. Designed to baffle rather
than inspire.

MOTHER MARGUERITA. Be a little careful, Don Hernando.
Do not forget we have a Bishop in our midst today.

SANTA CRUZ. Thank you, Mother Marguerita, but I am not
easily affronted, and Don Hernando is entitled to express his
reservations.

DON HERNANDO. As the only person here not bound in
servitude to Church or State, I rather think I am beholden to
stray beyond diplomacy.

The second part of his sermon was an outrage: a virulent
attack on Mexico. We are, it seems, a prayer away from
paganism, a sin away from our damnation. He paid no heed
at all to the presence of the Viceroy, but took advantage of
the pulpit to berate his governance at every turn.

VICEREINE. I would have stood and left had I believed that he would notice. The Archbishop does not wear his spectacles, I'm told, if there are women close at hand, so he is spared the sight of their corruption.

MOTHER MARGUERITA. Is that really so?

DON HERNANDO (*gazing at* ANGELICA). I would not deny my heart this sight for all the good in Christendom.

MOTHER MARGUERITA. Can that be so, my lord?

SANTA CRUZ. I fear there is some truth in it. I know he keeps no female servants in his house.

VICEREINE. He has declined all opportunity to meet me. Don Tomas has received him twice, but never at the palace.

DON HERNANDO. I wonder what he's so afraid of?

VICEREINE. Himself, I'll wager.

DON HERNANDO. Was he not of woman born?

VICEREINE. Perhaps he hatched. From an egg.

ANGELICA. Like a little bird.

DON HERNANDO. Precisely so.

VICEREINE. I was thinking of a lizard. There is something of the lizard in his look.

MOTHER MARGUERITA. Oh, dear.

DON HERNANDO. Sisters, I could never envy your incarceration, but at least it has delivered you today from the preaching of Aguiar y Seijas.

JUANA. Not entirely, Don Hernando. For he has sent a copy of his sermon to every convent in the land. For our instruction and improvement, I suppose.

MOTHER MARGUERITA. Yes. Though I have not had chance to read it yet.

SANTA CRUZ. But you have, sister?

JUANA. Yes, my lord.

DON HERNANDO. Of course she has.

SANTA CRUZ. And may I ask you what you thought of it?

VICEREINE. Yes, Sister Juana. Let us hear you put our great Archbishop in his place.

JUANA. Very well. Since I am commanded.

The first part, I found derivative. It departs very little from a Sermon of the Mandate delivered by a Jesuit in Lisbon more than forty years ago.

SANTA CRUZ. You are familiar with that sermon?

JUANA. I have a copy in my library.

MOTHER MARGUERITA. But the Archbishop is not a Jesuit.

DON HERNANDO. In all but name, it would appear.

JUANA. I have studied it at length and have questioned every one of its assertions. The Archbishop's interpretation of it, I disagree with more emphatically.

SANTA CRUZ. In what way?

JUANA. Aguiar y Seijas states that Christ loved Man more than He loved life, and that the greatest expression of His love therefore, was that, in dying on the cross, He absented himself from Man. To the Archbishop I would say, that Christ our Lord has never absented himself from us, for he remains present with us, in the transubstantiation of the Eucharist.

DON HERNANDO. Very good. That's very good.

JUANA. The Archbishop states that the second great expression of Christ's love for Man, was that He loved us without desiring that we love Him in return. Now whilst I have often eulogised on the supremacy of unrequited love in man, or woman, I would say to Aguiar y Seijas that we must not judge Christ by our own standards. For Christ did desire that we return His love; not for His own sake, but for ours. For in loving Christ we are loving God, and from love of God is born the love we have for all our fellow men and for ourselves.

MOTHER MARGUERITA. Yes.

VICEREINE. Excellent, Sister Juana.

JUANA. Then I would say this to Aguiar y Seijas. In my opinion, the greatest expressions, of Christ's love for us, are the gifts He does not grant us. I speak now of Christ as God. For in not granting us these gifts, He is releasing us from His hand and He is granting us our liberty.

SANTA CRUZ. Negative benefactions.

JUANA. Yes. It is no surprise to me that the Archbishop fails to consider this expression. For it is one which acknowledges, embraces rather, Man's free will as the ultimate reflection of divine grace.

DON HERNANDO (*smiling at* ANGELICA). Now we are confused again.

JUANA. God does not wish to deny us our humanity. He loves us for precisely what we are. If He were to grant us every blessing, every wish we crave, how then could we be human? How would we endeavour? Why? How would we learn, how would we hope, how would we care? How would we value anything? God wants us to be everything we can be. He wants us to strive, to achieve and sometimes, yes, to suffer. For we cannot value our success without the times that we have failed. We cannot love the gift of life without the knowledge we will die. We cannot cherish a newborn child unless we understand its frailty, nor can we look upon the blossom tree, and feel its beauty kiss our eyes with tears, unless we can remember it in wintertime. God sets us free that we might live. That is the glory and the grace.

MOTHER MARGUERITA. Beautiful. Quite beautiful.

JUANA. And in answer to the second part of the Archbishop's sermon, I would say this: we are not Spain, we are New Spain. We are not a country in decline, we are a country in ascendancy. We do not fear our past, we learn from it. Nor do we fear our volatility, for therein lies possibility and change. We do not wish to imitate the motherland, but to explore new ways of life, uncharted thought, and fresh philosophy. And with God's love, and with the guidance and new hope which we are blessed with in their Excellencies, there is nothing we cannot attain.

DON HERNANDO. Devastating.

VICEREINE. A comprehensive victory.

JUANA. But then I am only a woman. And what can the Archbishop learn from me?

Scene Two

The locutory. The bars have been pulled back. ANGELICA *is alone.*

JUANITA (*off*). Señorita Angelica! Where are you?

ANGELICA. Here.

JUANITA *enters.*

JUANITA. Now, what's that face for?

ANGELICA. Because they've gone. And I don't know when they'll come back again. Brigida says the Vicereine will have to be confined soon. None of them will come without her.

JUANITA. Oh, I don't know. You might see one of them sooner than you think.

ANGELICA. Who? Which one?

JUANITA. The one who pressed this note into my hand before he left, and whispered, 'Help me, Juanita,' in my ear. Which was not completely disagreeable.

ANGELICA. Who? You don't mean Don Hernando?

JUANITA. Don Hernando? Yes I do. And it's not just any old note either. Oh no. I recognise a love letter when I see one.

ANGELICA. Don Hernando is in love with you?

JUANITA. Not with me. It's not my name written on the front of it.

ANGELICA. Whose then? Whose?

JUANITA. Now let me see. Is it Sister Juana? No. Is it Brigida? But no. It's Señorita Angelica.

ANGELICA. Me? Me? Give it to me.

JUANITA *taunts her with the note*.

Juanita!

JUANITA *relinquishes the note*. ANGELICA *starts to read it*.

Oh, it cannot be. It cannot be. This can't be happening to me.

JUANITA. Let me see that.

She snatches the note.

'Angelica, my angel. How well they chose your name, for you are surely sent from Heaven.' Original. 'Pity me, save me, for since I came within your radiance, I cannot sleep, nor think, nor eat, for longing to be close to you.' Huh. He looks pretty well-fed to me. 'I have to see you on your own. Tell me how it might be done. Find a way, I beg of you. Write to me and tell me where and how and when and I will come to you, sweet love. I will come.' Well, he certainly didn't get Sister Juana to write that one.

ANGELICA. What am I going to do? I have to leave. I have to go to him at once.

JUANITA. Don't be silly, child. He doesn't want you to go running out of the convent. He doesn't want a scandal any more than you do.

ANGELICA. But how else can I see him on his own? Let me out of the garden door, Juanita. The one you use.

JUANITA. No, I will not.

ANGELICA. I could see him and then come back in. I promise I'd come back.

JUANITA. No. You're not setting foot outside these walls.

ANGELICA. But what will I do? He's desperate for me.

JUANITA. He's desperate for something.

ANGELICA. Juanita, please!

JUANITA *considers for a moment.*

JUANITA. I don't see why you shouldn't see him, just for a few minutes, mind. Have a little excitement, a little romance.

ANGELICA. Do you mean it?

JUANITA. We can see it as part of your instruction. I mean, how are you supposed to decide if you want to marry Jesus if you haven't got anyone to compare him with?

ANGELICA. Oh, thank you. Thank you. But how?

JUANITA. You leave that to me. Anything's possible in this place if you know the way things work.

Scene Three

SISTER JUANA*'s cell. Evening.* SISTER JUANA *is working at her desk.* SISTER SEBASTIANA *enters.*

SEBASTIANA. Bishop Santa Cruz, Sister Juana.

SANTA CRUZ *enters.*

SANTA CRUZ. Thank you, sister.

SISTER SEBASTIANA *leaves.*

I hope I do not disturb your work.

JUANA. No, my lord. I was hoping you would come.

SANTA CRUZ. I have been talking with Mother Marguerita for a while. I was about to leave when I remembered my promise to view your library.

JUANA. Yes. I am honoured.

She leaves her desk.

SANTA CRUZ. I am disturbing you.

JUANA. No. The muse is not with me today. The rhymes would not be captured. I was hoping you would come.

(*Inviting him to look.*) Please...

He begins to look at the books upon the shelves.

SANTA CRUZ. I feel as though I've walked into your mind.

JUANA. You will recognise many of the volumes.

SANTA CRUZ. Some of them. But my library is dedicated solely to theology.

JUANA. I like to think that mine is, in its way.

SANTA CRUZ. Mythology. Geometry. Astrology.

JUANA. Ah, but all those lesser disciplines I find essential to my understanding of the Scriptures.

SANTA CRUZ. So that's the only reason why you read them?

JUANA. That and my voracious and appalling curiosity.

I don't know what I'll do in years to come; there is no space left on the shelves. I have moved a number to the common room, but I hardly think it fair upon my sisters. Not that they complain. And more arrive each month from every corner of the globe.

SANTA CRUZ. And are they all permissible? These books which you are sent?

JUANA. All are interesting.

SANTA CRUZ. I ask only from appalling curiosity.

JUANA. I have received a certain number I would not openly display. Certain political and scientific theses.

I do not understand the fear some have, of reading words which might present a contradiction to their faith. I can only think their faith is weak. I can attempt to comprehend the movement of the planets, without I question it was God who made them.

Father Antonio would not agree with me. He once found an essay by Descartes on my desk. I thought he would expire. He forbade my reading for three months. I am more than careful now.

SANTA CRUZ. Plays. Essential to your understanding of the Scriptures?

JUANA. Essential to my understanding of the human heart. That is important too.

SANTA CRUZ. Judging from your play, I'd say you need no help with that.

JUANA. I have memory to draw upon. I was not born a nun.

He stares at her for a moment.

My lord, may I ask for your advice?

SANTA CRUZ. Of course.

JUANA. Father Antonio has asked me to stop writing.

SANTA CRUZ. 'Asked', you say? I thought it would have been an order.

JUANA. It was not.

SANTA CRUZ. And have you stopped writing, Sister Juana?

JUANA. As chance would have it, I have been offered only small and personal commissions of late. Nothing to warrant great attention. But no; I have not stopped writing.

Am I wrong? I would greatly value your opinion.

SANTA CRUZ. I was fascinated to hear you speaking on theology today.

JUANA. I hope you did not think me disrespectful.

SANTA CRUZ. A good argument deserves to be heard, whether it is made by a woman or a man. Unlike many of my brothers, I am not of the opinion that women should lead silent lives. We have been too quick to disregard the example of Saint Catherine. Of Saint Paula.

JUANA. That is what I always say.

SANTA CRUZ. At my school in Puebla, I allow several experienced and elderly sisters to instruct the girls. They do so very well.

JUANA. Yes, I have heard that.

SANTA CRUZ. I have also been confessor to a small number of mystic nuns. Whilst their visions, their insights are not reasoned, are purely sensual, shall we say, I encourage them and help them to write down everything they see and feel. And I distribute copies of their writings to my brothers, for I think that we can learn from them.

If I have never championed a nun who speaks upon theology, it is only because I never met with one who can. Until now.

The more I learn of you, the more I feel that it would be a tragedy were we to lose your voice, your intellect due to the excess stringency of one well-meaning man. I cannot counsel disobedience, but were I your confessor I would be urging you to write. To write what you want to write. To learn, to teach, to debate, to argue. To explore the very limits of your gift. I would not question the significance of what you had to say. And I would never, ever doubt you.

SISTER JUANA *is overwhelmed. A bell in the convent rings.*

You are called to vespers.

JUANA. Yes.

She kisses his sleeve. He kisses her hand, her head. It is unusual and highly charged intimacy.

SISTER SEBASTIANA *enters, but on seeing them, leaves again. They do not notice her.*

I wish it had been you. The new Archbishop.

SANTA CRUZ. Be patient. Be strong, Sister Juana. Go now. I will visit you again.

JUANA. I count upon it.

She leaves.

SANTA CRUZ. I was not born a priest. And she is soft and
warm beneath those clothes, and she is perfumed too. Why
should she be perfumed so? A Sister of the Church. Could it
have been for me? For me she bathed and touched her skin
with something so voluptuous? 'I was hoping you would
come.' My God, what rare temptation. All these years with
women at my feet and I have never reached for one. But she.
She. She is my match, in thought, in spirit and in deed. As
mindful of her reputation as I of mine. And if one day we
locked the door, why then… For shame; she has uncentred
me. Yet I am not inclined to still these new and lavish
rhythms in my heart.

Why should we not be allied, against the Archbishop and his
kind? A faction forged between the sheets. With secrets
shared. And dreams unleashed. What damage then could not
be done? I must to prayer, to set a little credit by for my
transgressions yet to come.

Scene Four

The locutory. The bars are in place. JUANITA *enters from the
cloister as* BRIGIDA *enters from the gate.*

JUANITA. Was that the bell, Brigida?

BRIGIDA. Don Hernando is at the gate. My mistress wants to
know if Sister Juana will see him.

JUANITA. She's been expecting him. He needs her help to
write a poem. I'll go and fetch her now if you will kindly
show him in.

BRIGIDA. 'Kindly'? What are you up to with your 'kindly'?
Why so suddenly polite?

JUANITA. But, Brigida, should I not be poilte to you? When I
am but a humble slave and you are a respected servant. And
so very senior in years?

BRIGIDA. Huh! Just go and get Sister Juana.

JUANITA goes. BRIGIDA exits to the gate. After a moment, JUANITA enters, leading ANGELICA, who is disguised as SISTER JUANA. She is wearing one of SISTER JUANA's habits, and a veil covers her face.

JUANITA. Sit down here. Don't think to stand, your lack of height betrays you.

ANGELICA. I won't.

JUANITA. Don't lift your veil, nor open up your mouth to speak unless you're quite alone with him.

ANGELICA. But how will he perceive it's me?

JUANITA. Because I warned him in the note I sent to him, of course.

ANGELICA. I see. This is a proper subterfuge. I think I shall faint with excitement.

JUANITA. Don't. For if you do, it means the end for both of us.

Ten minutes, not a moment more, and for that time I'll keep my mistress in her cell.

People are heard approaching.

Be silent now.

SISTER SEBASTIANA, DON HERNANDO *and* BRIGIDA *enter from the gate.*

DON HERNANDO. Ah, Juanita.

JUANITA. Sister Juana awaits you, Don Hernando.

DON HERNANDO. Excellent. That's excellent.

SEBASTIANA. Why does she wear her veil down?

JUANITA. Oh, that is easily explained. Last night at prayer she swore to spend this day in private contemplation and does not wish to look upon the world. Pity alone for Don Hernando's plight has drawn her forth to speak to him.

DON HERNANDO. I petitioned her remorselessly, for I am urgently in need of her assistance.

SEBASTIANA. Then I will leave you. Brigida will see you out when you have finished.

DON HERNANDO. Thank you, sister.

SISTER SEBASTIANA *exits to the cloister.*

JUANITA. And I will leave you too. I'm sure you wish to be alone for this short time agreed upon.

DON HERNANDO. I am obliged, Juanita. A little privacy would be most welcome.

BRIGIDA *does not leave, but settles in a chair close by.* JUANITA *rushes off to keep an eye on* SISTER JUANA.

Sister Juana, I will begin at once, if you'll allow, for here before you is a man so wild, so lost, so overwhelmed his heart can barely be contained within the confines of his form.

ANGELICA. Oh!

DON HERNANDO. Yes. I am in love. And there are those would say to you that I have been in love before, have sat here in this very room and claimed my heart is spoken for, would tell you that the Court is strewn, yes, littered with a history of my devoted protestations, yet I would beg you to believe that, this time, it is different. You do believe me, don't you?

ANGELICA. Yes. I mean... (*Nods.*)

DON HERNANDO. There is a girl, yet 'girl' is not enough: an angel, a deity, who with a single smile has touched the very centre of my soul. I never felt so potently my want of words, my lack of poetry, and I implore you, beg you please, become my voice, invoke your muse, make her conceive the vehemence of my passion.

Find the words to tell her she is bright and pure as mountain snow. Tell her that she is the light for whose sweet warmth I would forgo all power, all wealth, all rival charms. Tell her I would give my life to lie, one moment, in her arms.

BRIGIDA. Amen to that.

DON HERNANDO. Still here, Brigida?

BRIGIDA. Yes, good sir. What can I do for you?

DON HERNANDO. A glass of water, if I may? I feel a sudden thirst arise.

BRIGIDA. I'm not surprised. What need have you of poems, sir, when you can talk in such a way? But pardon me. I shall return.

She exits to the cloister. ANGELICA *lifts her veil.*

DON HERNANDO. Angelica. Angelica.

ANGELICA. Oh, Don Hernando!

DON HERNANDO. See how I tremble, how I quake to be, at last, so close to you. Oh, what a lovesick wretch am I. Give me your hand that I might kiss the open softness of your palm.

ANGELICA *puts her hand through the bars. He kisses it.*

ANGELICA. Ah!

DON HERNANDO. And now your lips that I might taste the honeyed nectar of their balm.

They kiss through the bars.

What joy.

ANGELICA. Now what? My nose? My knee?

DON HERNANDO. But no. Accept this gift from me.

He passes something through the bars.

ANGELICA. A ring.

DON HERNANDO. A promise that my love is true.

ANGELICA. A ring. For me. Oh, come here, you!

She reaches through the bars and pulls him towards her. They kiss. BRIGIDA *enters, unseen by them, and recognises* ANGELICA.

BRIGIDA *(aside)*. Dear Lord above, what's this I see?

She withdraws.

DON HERNANDO. I swear we'll be together soon.

ANGELICA. But how? Juanita will not let me out, I know she won't.

DON HERNANDO. I'll find a way. Just tell me that you'll come to me the moment that I send for you.

ANGELICA. I will. I will and happily.

DON HERNANDO. It is enough. Go now, before we are undone.

ANGELICA. Come for me soon.

DON HERNANDO. I will, my love. And all of Heaven shall be ours.

ANGELICA. Just one kiss more. I like it.

They kiss.

DON HERNANDO. And now be gone.

ANGELICA *exits to the cloister.*

(*Calling after her.*) My thanks, dear Sister Juana! My hopes are in your care!

BRIGIDA *enters.*

BRIGIDA. Your water, sir.

He takes the water from her.

DON HERNANDO. I am obliged, Brigida.

BRIGIDA. Off to write your verse, is she?

DON HERNANDO. The verse I hope will win my prize.

BRIGIDA. I hope you get what you deserve.

DON HERNANDO. Thank you, dear lady. So do I.

ACT THREE

Scene One

In the convent chapel, MOTHER MARGUERITA, SISTER
JUANA, SISTER SEBASTIANA *and other* NUNS *are
praying.*

ANGELICA *is also praying.*

The city bells begin to ring. The NUNS *continue with their
prayers.*

ANGELICA (*whispering*). Why are the bells ringing?

SEBASTIANA. Silence!

BRIGIDA *enters with a letter. The* SISTERS *reach the end
of their prayers.* BRIGIDA *hands the letter to* MOTHER
MARGUERITA, *who opens it.*

MOTHER MARGUERITA. Great news! The Lord be praised.
The Vicereine is delivered of a son.

ANGELICA. A son!

JUANA. But surely it's too soon?

MOTHER MARGUERITA. Yet all is well, and both are strong
and hearty. It's written here and in the Viceroy's hand.

JUANA. Thank God! Thank God!

MOTHER MARGUERITA. And there is more. For here is a
request for you, Sister Juana. He wishes you to write a play.
A play to grace the celebrations at the christening of his son.

JUANA. May I read it for myself?

MOTHER MARGUERITA *hands her the letter.*

MOTHER MARGUERITA. We reach new heights of honour.
Spain and half the world shall hear our convent's name.

ANGELICA. What will you write?

JUANA. That I cannot say. But there is very little time and so it will be short. But fitting. The best and greatest of my work, for I have never known before such joyous inspiration.

ANGELICA. Can I help you?

JUANA. With the copying, certainly.

MOTHER MARGUERITA. We will ensure you have the peace you need. Come. You should begin at once. And I will write an answer to the Viceroy, expressing all our thanks and love.

All leave, except SISTER SEBASTIANA *and* BRIGIDA.

BRIGIDA. Great news, then, mistress.

SEBASTIANA. Great news. Oh, yes. But which is greater? That the Viceroy of all Mexico has now an infant son and heir or that Sister Juana de la Cruz is asked to write another play? For which shall we give thanks? My God, my God, forgive me, for I will hate my way to Hell!

BRIGIDA. Mistress!

SEBASTIANA. No amount of scourging now, no sacrifice of flesh and blood can cleanse me of this poison. It is for her, for her that I am damned!

BRIGIDA. Oh, mistress, do not say so.

SEBASTIANA. What has she done that is so wonderful? What has she done for God that we should stand in awe of her? She fashions words and has an outward prettiness and so they flock and fawn on her as though she were divine. And we, I, who am so diligent, no, brilliant in the completeness of my faith, am overlooked as nothing, worse, am forced to be an acolyte, a servant at the court of her celebrity.

BRIGIDA. It is a shame upon the Church.

SEBASTIANA. She came from nothing. She does not even know her father's name. I am the daughter of a count. I could have danced at any court in any land and married where my favour fell. But no, no, I cannot be her equal.

BRIGIDA. Hush, mistress, now. Someone will hear.

SEBASTIANA. The Bishop of Puebla! Even he. A man I have admired so long. Even he is all for her and cannot see beyond her face.

BRIGIDA. It is unjust. But listen now.

SEBASTIANA. That all my hopes and childhood prayers should end in this. I do not want this. To live and die defined by this monstrosity!

BRIGIDA. Mistress, please. You'll make yourself unwell.

SEBASTIANA. There is no sickness worse than this. This sickness I will take beyond the grave.

BRIGIDA. But listen to me now. For I might have the wherewithal to cure you of your malady.

I'll prove to you that all is not as perfect as it might appear in Sister Juana's world.

SEBASTIANA. What do you mean? Tell me.

BRIGIDA. Not here, but in your cell. You shall lie down and hear my tale. And then, dear mistress, you may act upon it as you will.

Scene Two

The ARCHBISHOP's *office. The* ARCHBISHOP *is at work.* FATHER ANTONIO *enters.*

FATHER ANTONIO. You sent for me, Your Grace?

ARCHBISHOP. I hear the nun is writing once again.

FATHER ANTONIO. I wondered if that might not be the reason for my summons.

ARCHBISHOP. Did you? Well, now you may count prophecy amongst your many gifts.

FATHER ANTONIO. Your Grace, as regards the nun… as regards Sister Juana, I feel we have made significant and heartening progress. She is spending fewer hours now at her desk. Her latest undertaking, however, is a commission from the Viceroy.

ARCHBISHOP. I am aware of that.

FATHER ANTONIO. Which she could not possibly refuse without she cause extreme offence.

ARCHBISHOP. Censor it. I want it censored. The play will not take place.

FATHER ANTONIO. Censor it? Your Grace, I cannot censor it.

ARCHBISHOP. Cannot?

FATHER ANTONIO. I have not even read it yet. I do not think it finished. I highly doubt it will contain the merest hint of heresy. No, Your Grace. I will not censor it without good cause.

ARCHBISHOP. It is a play, and that is cause enough. That is your cause. A piece of decadence. Morally corrupt. Insidious, pernicious, self-regarding. I'll write a list, if you desire, of words with which you might condemn it.

There will be no more plays performed whilst I remain Archbishop. Be they written by nuns or priests or mountebanks. That is my decree, and I must trust you to enforce it.

FATHER ANTONIO. The Viceroy would consider it a personal affront.

ARCHBISHOP. And what of that? A personal affront? You have spent too long about the Court, Father Antonio. I might consider it a personal affront that I am not prevailed upon to christen this 'infante'. That Bishop Santa Cruz shall christen it, and not in the cathedral; within some palace chapel, where all the weight and wonder of the service is lost upon the populace.

FATHER ANTONIO. I did not know this.

ARCHBISHOP. No?

FATHER ANTONIO. Bishop Santa Cruz?

ARCHBISHOP. I might consider it a personal affront to receive a letter from Madrid suggesting I am overzealous in my ministry. I do not care. I am not so ingloriously vain as to believe my mewlings of humiliation should be of any import here. Nor will I shrink from any confrontation. 'He only is my rock and my salvation: He is my defense; I shall not be moved.'

FATHER ANTONIO. She will appeal. Of that I'm certain. She will send it to Madrid and look to higher authority than mine.

ARCHBISHOP. Then let her. Months will pass before she has her judgement. The celebrations will be long forgotten, and New Spain will be a different place. Censor it.

Scene Three

In the locutory. ANGELICA *is reading a note.* SISTER SEBASTIANA *and* BRIGIDA *enter and watch her from a distance.*

BRIGIDA. There she is. And with the very note. A young man brought it to the door ten minutes since. He told me it was from her father, but I know well her father's hand and it is not from him. Look – see how her face is shining now.

SEBASTIANA. Thank you, Brigida. You have done well.

BRIGIDA. What shall we do? Shall I fetch Sister Juana?

SEBASTIANA. No. Go now. Say nothing. I will deal with this myself. Go.

BRIGIDA. Well, if I must.

BRIGIDA *leaves.* SISTER SEBASTIANA *walks straight to* ANGELICA, *who sees her and turns pale.*

ANGELICA. Sister!

SEBASTIANA. Give it to me.

ANGELICA. What? I can't. I mean… It's private.

SEBASTIANA. Give it to me.

> ANGELICA *hands her the note*. SISTER SEBASTIANA
> *looks at the signature on it*.

ANGELICA. Please, I…

SEBASTIANA. Don Hernando.

ANGELICA. Oh no. Oh no. Oh, sister, please. Please don't tell
anyone. Please don't tell my aunt, I beg of you. I will do
anything. I love him. I cannot help myself. I love him.

> Please don't tell Sister Juana, I beg of you. I beg of you.

SEBASTIANA. Take your hands off me!

ANGELICA. Sister Sebastiana…

SEBASTIANA (*reading the note*). He wants to meet you.
Tonight. There is a servant in the kitchens who will let you
out of the garden door, 'if you give her this.' What's this?

> ANGELICA *holds out a coin*.

ANGELICA. He sent it with the note.

SEBASTIANA (*reading*). And she will let you in again when
you are done. Will she indeed? And what is it you mean to
do? When you meet this man?

ANGELICA. I do not know exactly. But he will hold me in his
arms. And he will kiss me. He loves me too.

> SISTER SEBASTIANA *thinks for a moment*.

SEBASTIANA. Well. I can see why you would want to go. To
be held. And kissed. I can understand that.

ANGELICA. Can you?

SEBASTIANA. Meet him. You must. And if this servant whom
he writes of is too afraid to help you, come to me and I will
let you through the door myself, and let you in when you are
'done'.

ANGELICA. Do you mean it? You are not…? You would not…?

SEBASTIANA. Trick you? I would not be so cruel. But do not
tell him that I know. Do not tell a living soul. Mother
Prioress would not understand.

ANGELICA. I won't. It is our secret. Did you love once, Sister
Sebastiana?

SEBASTIANA. Take this note and burn it. Dry your eyes.
Brush your hair.

ANGELICA. I will.

SEBASTIANA. Go now. And do not fear; Sister Juana will not
hear of this.

ANGELICA. Thank you. Thank you.

   ANGELICA *leaves*.

Scene Four

SISTER JUANA*'s cell*. SISTER JUANA *is writing*. JUANITA
enters.

JUANITA. Sister Juana!

JUANA. No. Later, Juanita. Close the door behind you.

JUANITA. But you will want to hear this. I have just come
from the square. They've made a fire there. They are burning
books.

JUANA. What do you mean? Who are?

JUANITA. Priests. They're throwing books onto the flames.
Everyone is watching.

JUANA. What books? From where?

JUANITA. From the stalls. From the traders' shops.

   MOTHER MARGUERITA *enters, followed by* FATHER
   ANTONIO.

JUANA. Mother, have you heard this?

Father Antonio.

MOTHER MARGUERITA. We need to speak with you. Leave us please, Juanita.

JUANITA *leaves*.

JUANA. She tells me there are priests in the square, and that they are burning books.

FATHER ANTONIO. Yes. The Archbishop feels that there are too many books of a secular nature circulating through the city. He has asked that the traders surrender to us books of poetry or plays.

JUANA. To burn? You are burning books?

FATHER ANTONIO. And we are then replacing them with copies of religious texts. Words to truly feed the soul.

MOTHER MARGUERITA. Then there is purpose in it.

FATHER ANTONIO. Great purpose.

JUANA. And what if they refuse? What if these traders will not give up their books?

FATHER ANTONIO. There is one text in particular, which will, I think, prove salutary – *The Consolation of the Poor*. Fifteen hundred volumes arrived this week from Spain. A concise and simple treatise on the necessity of charity.

JUANA. You do not agree with this.

FATHER ANTONIO. We mean to bring the people's thoughts back to the founding tenets of the faith.

JUANA. You do not agree with this.

FATHER ANTONIO. The Archbishop has declared a war on decadence. It is a war I welcome, a war long overdue, which cannot be successfully waged from pulpit or confessional but must be taken to the streets. Measures must be taken. Visible and striking measures which the Archbishop is best placed to identify. I accept that now wholeheartedly.

MOTHER MARGUERITA. Sister Juana...

JUANA. So why are you here? (*Indicating her books*.) For these?

FATHER ANTONIO. It has not yet come to that.

JUANA. Yet?

FATHER ANTONIO. I have come to ask you to set aside the play on which you're working.

If you finish it, I will be forced to censor it.

JUANA. I have to finish it. It is a commission from the Viceroy. It is soon to be performed.

FATHER ANTONIO. It cannot be performed. The Archbishop has declared that no more plays will be performed in Mexico.

JUANA. I think the Viceroy will decide what can or cannot be performed within his palace. It is his palace after all. It is his country.

FATHER ANTONIO. It is God's country. First and foremost, it is God's country.

JUANA. On what grounds would you censor it? It is a touching tale of love and honour. And those who are good and true prevail.

FATHER ANTONIO. I will censor it. That is all.

JUANA. I will oppose you. The Vicereine will oppose you.

MOTHER MARGUERITA. Sister Juana…

FATHER ANTONIO. To no avail.

MOTHER MARGUERITA. Sister Juana, please. We cannot have the Inquisition here. I will write to the Viceroy. I am certain he will understand your position. For the sake of your sisters, of the order which you serve, please do not bring the Inquisition here.

JUANA. Well, then. It does not matter. I had hardly started, and it was not good. (*Holding it out to him*.) Take it. It is the only copy. Put it on your fire.

FATHER ANTONIO. No. Keep it. Lock it away.

JUANA. I can no longer confess to you, Your Reverence. Mother Prioress, I am in need of a new Father Confessor.

MOTHER MARGUERITA. No, sister. Don't...

FATHER ANTONIO. Thank you, Mother Marguerita, but it is as I expected.

MOTHER MARGUERITA. But...

FATHER ANTONIO. It is, perhaps, the wisest course. With all these years behind us, I am perhaps too close to properly guide Sister Juana. It is as I expected.

(*To* SISTER JUANA.) God bless you, child.

He leaves. MOTHER MARGUERITA *follows him out.*

Scene Five

The locutory. SISTER SEBASTIANA *enters from the gate, with* BISHOP SANTA CRUZ.

SEBASTIANA. Is Sister Juana expecting you, my lord?

SANTA CRUZ. She wrote a letter asking me to come to her. So, yes, I think I am 'expected'.

SEBASTIANA. Pardon me. I meant no disrespect. It's only that for some days now, she has refused all visitors.

SANTA CRUZ. She will not refuse me.

SEBASTIANA. No, my lord. Of course. Please come this way and I will...

SISTER SEBASTIANA *suddenly stops. She becomes agitated and her expression is one of terror.*

Oh no. Oh no. Not now.

SANTA CRUZ. What is it? What ails you, sister?

SEBASTIANA. It is nothing, my Lord. Ah! Forgive me.

SANTA CRUZ. Take my arm. Lean on me.

SEBASTIANA. No! No, I will recover presently.

SANTA CRUZ. Sit down a moment then, or you will fall.

SISTER SEBASTIANA *is staring wildly.*

SEBASTIANA. It cannot be. No. I will not see it. I'm here. This is the convent. This is the ground.

Oh, God! God help me!

SANTA CRUZ. What are you seeing, sister? Speak to me.

SEBASTIANA. I am in a city. It is a city I do not recognise. The streets are sad. So sad and desolate. There are hardly any houses. The only ones that I can see are so poor, so derelict it hurts my heart to look at them. The light is dim. There are men passing by. They are very tall. They speak a language I do not know.

SANTA CRUZ. Have courage, sister.

SEBASTIANA. There is a fountain. The road is wide. There are some women there. They are washing clothes. Their heads are covered. It looks like they have come from mass. I cannot see their faces. She is turning to me. Oh, no! Oh, no! It is the Devil. Oh, God help me! God help me! God help me!

It has gone. It has passed.

SANTA CRUZ. What did the Devil look like? Quick, while it is in your mind.

SEBASTIANA. Too terrible to contemplate. His eyes were yellow, and at the centre, slits of black. His nose was long and pointed at the tip. His ears were pointed too.

SANTA CRUZ. How long have you been having visions?

SEBASTIANA. A week. Ten days, perhaps. No more. I do not know why they began. At night I am besieged by them. But never have I had one in the daylight until now.

SANTA CRUZ. Who have you told of this?

SEBASTIANA. No one.

SANTA CRUZ. What is your name?

SEBASTIANA. Sebastiana.

SANTA CRUZ. These visions are significant, Sister Sebastiana. God speaks to us by means of such imaginings. You must bring them to me. Share them with me and I will help you. We will record them and examine them minutely.

SEBASTIANA. I...

SANTA CRUZ. Who is your Father Confessor? I will speak to him.

SEBASTIANA. No. Thank you, my lord. I am humbled by your attention, but I will talk to my own confessor, I think.

SANTA CRUZ. But why? I have had three mystics in my care. There is no priest in Mexico so skilled as I to manage such a gift.

SEBASTIANA. I know, my lord, but...

SANTA CRUZ. But what? Are you afraid of me? Speak to me, sister.

SEBASTIANA. It's nothing.

SANTA CRUZ. What is nothing?

SEBASTIANA. It's only what Sister Juana said.

My lord, I am alarmed by any strain of intimacy. I could not...

SANTA CRUZ. What did Sister Juana say?

What did Sister Juana say?

SEBASTIANA. When all of us were gathered in the common room, she said... she said you touched her... and that you wanted certain things of her.

I am not as open as my sister. And if you... I would not...

SANTA CRUZ *turns away for a few moments. He is rigid with shock and anger. He recovers himself.*

SANTA CRUZ. I am only asking that you share your visions with me. That you allow me to interpret them and put them to good use.

SEBASTIANA. Yes.

SANTA CRUZ. I believe there was a reason that you had that vision in my sight. God wanted me to witness it.

SEBASTIANA. Yes.

SANTA CRUZ. He wanted me to help you. But if you feel you cannot trust my care…

SEBASTIANA. No. I do. I will, my lord. For what you say is right. Why else would my visions have crept beyond the boundaries of night-time? I will forget those words she said, for they were wicked words.

SANTA CRUZ. They were.

SEBASTIANA. I trust in you. And on my knees, I beg your counsel and support.

SANTA CRUZ. Then we shall do great work. God's work.

SEBASTIANA. Yes. Oh yes.

SANTA CRUZ. I will come to you tomorrow and we shall begin. Now, I must see Sister Juana.

SEBASTIANA. My lord, you will not…

SANTA CRUZ. I have no wish to cause unnecessary discord.

SEBASTIANA. Thank you.

SANTA CRUZ. Now take me to her, if you please.

SISTER JUANA*'s cell.* SISTER JUANA *is praying.* SISTER SEBASTIANA *enters with* BISHOP SANTA CRUZ.

SEBASTIANA. Bishop Santa Cruz, Sister Juana.

SISTER SEBASTIANA *leaves.*

JUANA. I knew you would come. Thank you, my lord.

SANTA CRUZ. I came as soon as I was able. What news?

JUANA. None but what I wrote to you.

SANTA CRUZ. No word yet from the Viceroy?

JUANA. No. Mother Marguerita sent the letter days ago, but he has not replied.

SANTA CRUZ. He must consider, I expect, what action he might take.

JUANA. I doubt he has even read it yet.

SANTA CRUZ. And Father Antonio?

JUANA. Father Antonio is gone, my lord. And I will never see him more.

SANTA CRUZ. Perhaps that is a good thing.

JUANA. But it is not. It is not a good thing. For I am left like this.

I am so angry. I am so angry. And most of all I am angry with myself, because I cannot drive his voice out of my head. So often in the past he has given me good counsel. Sometimes I have rejected what he has had to say to me, but then, in time, I have come to understand that he was right.

SANTA CRUZ. You think he is right?

JUANA. What if he is? I do not think he's right, but who am I to say that? Who am I to question him? Or the Archbishop? I appall myself. If they are so convinced of what is right for Mexico, for me, they in all their wisdom, how do I dare to doubt it? I do not even move amongst the world. What do I know?

Forgive me. I am not as I should be.

And I am angry with him. For at the very least he has left me utterly bewildered and utterly exposed. He always told me that my talent was a gift from God, and that I should embrace it, to the the glory of His name. But now it seems my talent is a sordid thing, a thing infectious from which the people must be saved. And I am left like this. And I cannot write.

SANTA CRUZ. What does it tell you of the man, this sudden change of heart? It tells me he is fallible. Weak, even. As likely to be right as wrong at any given time. Who knows to what we should attribute it? Perhaps he has some inward doubts he feels he cannot master, and looks therefore to those who deal in certainty. Perhaps he is ambitious still. Political. For there are churchmen who are both of these.

Whatever the cause of it might be, I do not think you should allow it to completely rearrange your world.

JUANA. You do not think he's right?

SANTA CRUZ. There will be no books burnt in Puebla. That I can promise you. And whilst I cannot mount an open challenge to the Archbishop's authority, I mean to do everything I can to call his judgement into question.

I am surprised at you. But then again, perhaps this was inevitable. He has been your confessor since you were a child, has he not?

JUANA. Since I was fifteen.

He would not take the play. It was as though a part of him still felt there was some value in my work.

SANTA CRUZ. And are you quite sure you will not finish it?

JUANA. No. Even as I held it out, I prayed he would not take it. And now I cannot help but hope that when the Vicereine is recovered, she will intervene and insist that it be finished and insist it be performed.

SANTA CRUZ. Good. And there are others too, I'm sure, who would support you. Come now. Write to all your learned friends abroad. Announce how you are persecuted and by whom.

JUANA. I will. Yes. You think I should? I will.

SANTA CRUZ. The critique I heard you once deliver, of the Archbishop's sermon, did you ever write it down?

JUANA. No, my lord. I would not dare submit such thoughts to paper.

SANTA CRUZ. It put his reasoning to shame. I would like to reacquaint myself with your arguments and use them to our advantage. If I may? Would you write it down and send it to me?

JUANA. Of course.

SANTA CRUZ. Only I would ever see what you had written.

JUANA. I'm sure I can remember it. It will not take me long.

SANTA CRUZ. Excellent. Take heart, beautiful Juana. We may derive some pleasure yet from our campaign.

He moves to leave. She kneels and clutches his sleeve. Kisses it.

JUANA. Thank you. Thank you.

My lord, I am in need of a new confessor. There is no one who understands me so well as you.

SANTA CRUZ. I think I understand you far too well.

JUANA. You will not do it?

SANTA CRUZ. We must not signal our alliance. I will think of someone suitable.

JUANA. Very well. Though I am mourning even now, the hours we would have had together.

SANTA CRUZ. And I.

Goodnight, Sister Juana.

JUANA. Goodnight.

He leaves.

Scene Six

In the locutory. MOTHER MARGUERITA *is reading a letter.* BISHOP SANTA CRUZ *enters, on his way to the gate.*

MOTHER MARGUERITA. My lord. Have you come from Sister Juana?

SANTA CRUZ. Yes. And offered her my loyalty.

MOTHER MARGUERITA. I'm glad. For she will soon have greater need of it. A letter from the Viceroy has arrived. They are to leave New Spain.

SANTA CRUZ. That is unexpected news.

MOTHER MARGUERITA. He asked to be recalled, it seems. He wants his son to grow up with the King.

SANTA CRUZ. And Mexico is cast aside.

MOTHER MARGUERITA. It is a dreadful blow. For Sister Juana most of all. To lose good Father Antonio, and now the Vicereine too.

SANTA CRUZ. Yes.

MOTHER MARGUERITA. This news should not be kept from her.

I thank God that she can count upon your patronage, my lord.

She leaves.

SANTA CRUZ. Here are changes, Santa Cruz. And yet the timing is not so amiss and things may fall out well for me. Don Tomas gone, it will be Aguiar y Seijas who is the first, the sole authority. They may create him Viceroy; the offices have been conjoined before, and there's an end to all my plans for pitting Church and Crown. I must move towards him then; make for the shelter of his throne and cling to it until the quakes have passed. And by God's Grace, I have the nun to open up a path for me, for now I know how free she makes with my good name, I'll suffer no compunction in destroying hers. What, did she think me desperate? Another panting fool to be castrated by her pen? Well, let her learn the cost of vanity. I'll offer up her heart to him.

ACT FOUR

Scene One

SISTER JUANA*'s cell.* SISTER JUANA *is writing.*
ANGELICA *is standing at the window, singing quietly. All the light has gone from her.*

JUANA. Hush, Angelica. If you must sing, at least go to another room.

ANGELICA. I don't want to be alone.

JUANA. But I do.

> ANGELICA *is quiet for a moment, but then begins to sing again. She stops suddenly.*

ANGELICA. If I am a child, Juana, can I go to Hell?

JUANA. Yes, is the simple answer. And I will send you there myself if you don't grant me peace. What ails you?

ANGELICA. I cannot say.

JUANA. Then come here and seal these letters for me. At least be useful if you cannot leave me be.

Voices are heard outside the door.

MOTHER MARGUERITA (*off*). I will see her at once.

JUANITA (*off*). But she does not wish to be disturbed.

Mother…

MOTHER MARGUERITA (*off*). Out of my way!

> MOTHER MARGUERITA *enters, followed by* JUANITA.

JUANA. Mother?

MOTHER MARGUERITA. How could you? How could you do this?

She brandishes a printed document.

JUANA. What? What is that?

MOTHER MARGUERITA. How could you be so reckless? So selfish?

JUANA. I don't understand. What is that?

MOTHER MARGUERITA. You know exactly what it is.

JUANA. But I do not. Show it to me, please.

MOTHER MARGUERITA *hands her the document.*

(*Reading.*) 'A letter, worthy of the wisdom of Athena, by Sister Juana Inés de la Cruz, a professed nun in the Most Spiritual Convent of San Jerónimo…'

MOTHER MARGUERITA. To criticise the Archbishop's work so openly. With such disdain.

SISTER JUANA *reads the document.*

JUANA. Where did you get this?

MOTHER MARGUERITA. It was delivered to the gate. And is being delivered to every monastery and convent in the land. It will be in *his* hands by now.

JUANA. This cannot be.

MOTHER MARGUERITA. Why do you pretend to such amazement? You wrote it. Or do you mean to deny that?

JUANA. I…

MOTHER MARGUERITA. And who is this Sister Filotea? Why did you send it to her? Who is she?

JUANA (*reading*). No… I do not know a Sister Filotea.

MOTHER MARGUERITA *snatches the document back.*

MOTHER MARGUERITA (*reading*). 'Written to and published by Sister Filotea de la Cruz, her most studious follower in the Convent of the Holy Trinity in Puebla.' One of your correspondents, I assume?

JUANA. My God. My God.

SISTER JUANA *collapses to the floor.*

JUANITA. Mistress!

MOTHER MARGUERITA. Oh, get up! Get up! You have brought us all to shame. It is the end of everything. For all of us.

JUANA. It's him.

JUANITA. Who? What do you mean, mistress?

JUANA. Bishop Santa Cruz. Sister Filotea de la Cruz. Of Puebla. It must be him, for it was him I sent it to.

MOTHER MARGUERITA. What madness are you talking now?

JUANA. I have to see him. Send for him.

JUANITA. He's here. Bishop Santa Cruz? He's with Sister Sebastiana. Or he was not long ago.

JUANA *takes the document back. She leaves the room.*

MOTHER MARGUERITA. Where are you going? Sister Juana? Sister Juana?

All follow her off.

Scene Two

SISTER SEBASTIANA*'s cell.* SISTER SEBASTIANA *is recalling a vision.* BISHOP SANTA CRUZ *is listening.*

SEBASTIANA. Her hair was lovely, great waves of it coming down her divine face, so graceful, so decorous, and all tied back around her neck. I knew at once it was Our Lady. She was exquisite. She emanated happiness. I feel her warmth about me still.

SISTER JUANA *enters.* MOTHER MARGUERITA *and* JUANITA *appear behind her.* BISHOP SANTA CRUZ *only glances up, and then continues.*

SANTA CRUZ. Was Christ with her?

SEBASTIANA. Yes. A child upon her shoulder.

SANTA CRUZ. The left shoulder?

SEBASTIANA. Yes. Close to her heart. There was such radiance about His face, and His eyes were bathed in silver tears.

JUANA. I need to speak to you.

BRIGIDA *enters from within*.

BRIGIDA. What are you doing in here? Oh – forgive me, Mother.

MOTHER MARGUERITA. Do not fret, Brigida, we are leaving. Come away, Sister Juana.

SISTER JUANA *does not move*.

SANTA CRUZ (*to* SISTER SEBASTIANA). Rest a moment, sister. You have earned it.

SEBASTIANA. Thank you, my lord.

SANTA CRUZ. What is it you wish to say to me, Sister Juana?

JUANA. What is this?

She holds up the document.

SANTA CRUZ. Ah, yes. Good. The printing did not take as long as I expected.

JUANA. You published it.

SANTA CRUZ. Yes. You seem surprised.

JUANA. It was for your eyes alone. You knew that. You said that, and I agreed with you.

SANTA CRUZ. That was not my understanding. It's strange, is it not, how words exchanged between two people can be construed by each so differently?

It is no more than we discussed.

JUANA. And what is this? These words by Sister Filotea de la Cruz? That is you?

SANTA CRUZ. Yes. I could hardly put my name to it. Some will understand the ruse and some will not. I thought it quite in keeping with the spirit of the thing. It is but a little mischief after all.

JUANA. But you admonish me. In this passage you have written in her name. You publically admonish me.

SANTA CRUZ. That is hardly an admonishment. I suggest you might consider opening your Bible from time to time. Only that.

I could not waste the opportunity of reminding all your readers of their duty. I'm sure you will have noticed that I also praise your gifts. 'A letter worthy of the wisdom of Athena.' If that is not praise then I do not know what is.

JUANA. Why have you done this? How have I offended you that you should now deceive me in this way?

SANTA CRUZ. Deceive you?

JUANA. You know that you are lying. This is unspeakable duplicity.

SANTA CRUZ. Do not forget whom you address.

JUANA. You have betrayed me. And used me. They will call this heresy.

SANTA CRUZ. I think not.

JUANA. They will seize on this and they will call it heresy and they will finish me.

MOTHER MARGUERITA. Sister Juana…

JUANA. Is that what you want?

SANTA CRUZ. Be silent. In God's name, be silent. Is there no limit to your vanity? Do you really think yourself so notable, so critical, that I would spend the briefest portion of my time considering your fate?

(*Indicating the document.*) As for that, it is done now. It is a piece of paper. The impudent impressions of a wayward nun. And if you cannot stand by what it says, you should not have written it.

Take it. And read the warning offered you by Sister Filotea.
It is given in good faith. For those negative benefactions
which you write about so assuredly apply to you as well.
And if you do not nurture more humility, you may receive
the greatest blessing yet, and find yourself rejected at the
Gates of Heaven.

JUANA. I will not let this pass.

SANTA CRUZ (*shouting suddenly and ferociously*). Get out!

We have important work to do.

MOTHER MARGUERITA. Come away now, Sister Juana.

JUANA. You do not know me yet.

MOTHER MARGUERITA. Come away! For pity's sake, have
you not done enough?

SISTER JUANA *leaves. All withdraw, leaving* SISTER
SEBASTIANA *and* BISHOP SANTA CRUZ *alone again.*

Scene Three

The sound of heavy rain can be heard.

The ARCHBISHOP's *palace.* BISHOP SANTA CRUZ *is
waiting in the anteroom. After a moment,* FATHER ANTONIO
enters from the ARCHBISHOP's *room.*

SANTA CRUZ. Ah. Father Antonio.

FATHER ANTONIO. He will see you now.

SANTA CRUZ. I assume his mood is less than good.

FATHER ANTONIO. He knows it's you, Santa Cruz. This
Sister Filotea. Who else would have the wherewithal to
publish such a thing?

SANTA CRUZ. I'm sure he does. It was always my intention
that he should. And soon he'll know and understand exactly
why I did it.

FATHER ANTONIO. Oh yes. I'm sure if anyone can execute such leaps of plausibility, it's you.

SANTA CRUZ. Meaning what?

FATHER ANTONIO *starts to leave*.

Another time, then.

FATHER ANTONIO *turns back*.

FATHER ANTONIO. What did you say to her? To make her write a thing so dangerous?

SANTA CRUZ. Very little, as it happens. The impetus was hers.

FATHER ANTONIO. I can't believe that. She has never before committed such thoughts to paper.

SANTA CRUZ. But she has had the thoughts. And spoken them aloud, as well, to anyone who'd listen, in that salon of subversion which is her cell. I have done what was required and I have drawn her out. My condemnation of her arrogance is there for all the world to see. The Archbishop, moreover, has the opportunity, the deserved opportunity to counter her attack and to make of her a notable example. For she is the embodiment of all that is sick in Mexico, and Church and Empire will be much relieved to see her overcome.

FATHER ANTONIO. I will not bring her before the Inquisition, if that is what you plan. To write the letter was misguided, reprehensible, yes, but she stops short of questioning or criticising articles of faith.

SANTA CRUZ. But the letter is not all. Is it? I have been made aware of certain facts about the direction of her studies, shall we say, and about her moral conduct which would bear further scrutiny. I'm sure you know the kind of thing to which I am referring.

FATHER ANTONIO. No, I do not.

SANTA CRUZ. Really? But then you would have to say that. For if you knew, yet failed to act, searching questions would be asked about your motives, and the condition of your soul.

FATHER ANTONIO. I have done more than anyone, for many years, to caution her and bring her into line.

SANTA CRUZ. Too slow. Too little, Father.

I mustn't keep him waiting. If you will excuse me.

He exits to the ARCHBISHOP'*s office.*

Scene Four

In the locutory. The bars are drawn. BRIGIDA *is cleaning.*
ANGELICA *enters.*

ANGELICA. Is it true, Brigida? Is the Viceroy coming?

BRIGIDA. Yes. And for the last time, God willing.

This rain! When will it stop? I never knew rain like it.

SISTER SEBASTIANA *enters from the gate.*

SEBASTIANA (*to* BRIGIDA). Be quick and fetch the sisters. They are approaching.

BRIGIDA. Yes, mistress.

BRIGIDA *exits to the cloister.*

ANGELICA. Sister Sebastiana, may I speak to you?

SEBASTIANA. Not now.

ANGELICA. But it's about him. Please.

SEBASTIANA. What? Be quick.

ANGELICA. The last time that I went to meet him, he didn't come. I waited outside the garden but he didn't come.

SEBASTIANA. Something held him at the palace. Clearly.

ANGELICA. But I have written notes to him and he has not replied.

SEBASTIANA. This is none of my concern.

ANGELICA. But I have to speak to him. Will he come today? (*Holding out a note.*) Give this to him, please. If he comes, you will have more chance than I, for I will not be close to him.

SEBASTIANA. No. Do you really think that I have time for this? I am a messenger of God, and filled each night with revelations. I should not be put upon to do my duty at the gate, let alone be burdened by your pitiful petitions.

ANGELICA. I am afraid.

SEBASTIANA. Do not speak of this to me again. Speak to Sister Juana.

ANGELICA. Sister Juana?

SEBASTIANA. She is so wise, and sure to give you good advice.

SISTER SEBASTIANA *exits to the gate. The* SISTERS, *including* SISTER JUANA, *enter from the cloister, led by* MOTHER MARGUERITA. ANGELICA *goes to stand with them.*

The VICEROY, VICEREINE, DON HERNANDO *and* MEMBERS OF THE COURT *enter from the gate, led by* SISTER SEBASTIANA, *who then joins her* SISTERS *behind the bars.*

VICEROY. Mother Marguerita, we have come to bid you sad farewell.

MOTHER MARGUERITA. Your Excellency. We pray for you and ask the Lord to keep you safe upon your journey to the motherland. May he hold you always in his care – and the Vicereine, and your little son.

VICEROY. We thank you with all our heart.

MOTHER MARGUERITA. You have not brought the infant? We all had hopes of seeing him?

VICEROY. There is some talk of sickness on the streets. And with the rain so merciless we did not wish to bring him forth.

MOTHER MARGUERITA. I understand.

VICEROY. It is with a heavy heart we find that we must leave these shores at such an inauspicious time. But Mexico is strong, and fortified a thousandfold by the power of your devotion.

MOTHER MARGUERITA. You are too kind.

VICEREINE. Mother Marguerita, we will always think with warm affection of you and all the sisters here. Many of our sweetest hours have been enjoyed within these walls.

MOTHER MARGUERITA. Thank you, Your Excellency.

VICEREINE. Now, if you will permit, I must request some private time with Sister Juana, in her cell.

MOTHER MARGUERITA. I'm afraid that is not possible. The law of the cloister must be observed. That is my instruction.

VICEREINE. Then I will pass beyond the grille, at least.

MOTHER MARGUERITA. No. I must regretfully deny that.

JUANA. Your Excellency, the bars will not deter us. We can speak quite well, I think, in spite of them.

VICEREINE. Very well. Though it is not as I would wish.

SISTER JUANA *moves to one end of the bars. The* VICEREINE *goes to her.*

JUANA. Do not be distressed.

VICEREINE. There was so much I wished to say to you.

JUANA. And I to you. Pretend they are not here. Come, take my hand.

How is the baby?

VICEREINE. They keep you like a prisoner.

JUANA. How is the baby?

VICEREINE. He is well. And beautiful. Even in my dreams I did not know the joy, the peace that I would feel to look upon his gentle face. I wanted you to see him.

JUANA. I know. I have a poem for him.

VICEREINE. Juana, come with us. Come with us. I would take care of you. You would want for nothing.

JUANA. Come with you?

VICEREINE. There are convents in Madrid. In Seville, if you prefer. You need not renounce your vows. I would find a place for you, if that is what you wished.

JUANA. I can't. I have to stay.

VICEREINE. Juana, there are rumours. They mean to bring you before the Inquisition.

JUANA. I know. And I will not be seen to run away.

VICEREINE. Oh, Juana, please.

JUANA. For what then would they say of me? That I knew the wrong I'd done and could not face their questions? That I was not a holy nun, in truth, but only used this order for the privilege it offered me. That I abandoned Mexico and all my sisters.

VICEREINE. You are not responsible for Mexico. As for your 'sisters', I should say they might be glad to see you gone.

Forgive me.

JUANA. I have to stay, Maria.

Take this, please.

She passes a portfolio through the bars.

In it there are copies of my poems – the ones I would wish seen. And my essays. My play. I beg you, keep them safe for me.

VICEREINE. I will do more than that. I will have them published, and spread through every realm.

JUANA. Then take this too. Let it be seen.

She passes one more document through the bars.

VICEREINE. What is it?

JUANA. My response to Bishop Santa Cruz. For what can we women do but answer? It is an explanation of myself. A defence of my right to learn and read and write and speak. Of every woman's right to have a voice within the world. Within the Church. The other copy I have sent to him. It is the stuff of my defence. I wish it to be seen.

VICEREINE. It will be. Even by the King. I will speak to him as soon as I am able. They will not dare to persecute you.

JUANA. Thank you.

VICEREINE. Juana...

JUANA. When do you leave?

VICEREINE. Tomorrow. The valleys are flooding. They say the roads will soon be lost, so we must leave at once.

JUANA. Then go. And godspeed. And know you never had a truer friend, nor one who loved you half as well as I. Please. Go.

The VICEREINE *turns back to her husband.*

VICEREINE. Come. I am ready now.

DON HERNANDO. And I must also say goodbye.

MOTHER MARGUERITA. You are leaving, too, Don Hernando?

DON HERNANDO. Yes. Don Tomas claims that he has need of me, though I cannot think for what. And I have recently inherited extensive lands in Spain which warrant my attention.

Farewell, Sister Juana. Sisters all. It has been a pleasure I will not forget.

JUANA. Farewell, Don Hernando.

The COURT *leave.* BRIGIDA *shows them to the gate.*

ANGELICA. No!

MOTHER MARGUERITA. Señorita! Control yourself. Come, sisters, let us pray for them.

The NUNS *exit towards the cloister.* ANGELICA *remains standing at the bars.* JUANITA *goes to her.*

JUANITA. Tell me you don't still think of him. Men like that were made to come and go. You'll soon forget him.

She goes after the NUNS. ANGELICA *remains.*

Scene Five

SISTER JUANA*'s cell. Outside, the rain is still pouring, and thunder can be heard.* JUANITA *enters and* SISTER JUANA *rushes to meet her.*

JUANA. Is it true?

JUANITA. Yes, mistress. The streets are full of water. Past my ankles – look.

JUANA. But this is dreadful.

JUANITA. I dared not go beyond the square. I saw a house collapse. One moment it was there, the next it buckled, sank and fell and there was nothing left of it. A moment's dust, then even that was swallowed by the rain.

JUANA. Sit down, let me help you. You should dry your feet.

JUANITA. People are gathering on the streets. No one trusts the walls to stand. The city gates are closed, but nothing holds the water back.

JUANA. But the Viceroy? Maria? Did they have chance to leave?

JUANITA. Someone said they left at dawn, before the water rose too high. Hurried off without a trumpet's call, or any crowd to wish them well.

JUANA. That matters not. Pray God they make it safe to Veracruz.

JUANITA. And they did well to leave today, for there is talk of riots.

JUANA. Riots?

JUANITA. The granaries are empty. That's the rumour passing round. No one gave a thought to this. And now the crops are ruined. Animals are washed away. The people will be starving soon.

JUANA. I wonder how my mother fares.

The bell to the convent gate is heard.

JUANITA. The bell. Do you hear? A poor soul seeking shelter, I suppose. There will be many more of those before the day is out.

She goes to the window and looks out.

Why is this happening?

JUANA. I cannot say.

JUANITA. Look at the sky. What sort of sky is that? That sickly glow, like yellow wax?

JUANA. It does seem strange.

JUANITA. The sun is ailing. Oh, mistress, I'm afraid.

MOTHER MARGUERITA *enters, with* SISTER SEBASTIANA, BRIGIDA *and* NUNS *behind her.*

MOTHER MARGUERITA. Sister Juana. The Archbishop has come. He has asked for you.

JUANA. He has come here?

JUANITA. No. Don't go to him.

MOTHER MARGUERITA. A delegation at the gate. He will not look upon us. He is in the locutory.

JUANA. He waited only till they'd left the city.

JUANITA. Don't go to him, mistress.

JUANA. Prepare some things for me, Juanita. My Bible. My plainest habit. Just in case.

MOTHER MARGUERITA. Sister Juana…

JUANA. Don't be alarmed, Mother. I will tell him I at all times disobeyed you.

Scene Six

In the locutory. The ARCHBISHOP *is sitting with his back to the bars.* SISTER JUANA *enters from the cloister.*

JUANA. Your Grace?

I am Sister Juana Inés de la Cruz.

I'm told you wish to see me.

ARCHBISHOP. I have no wish to see you. But I would speak some words to you.

JUANA. There is something I would like to say, Your Grace. If you'll allow it?

Whilst I stand by every argument I made against your sermon of the mandate, it was never my intention to commit my thoughts to paper, nor to have them published and distributed about the city. It was never my desire to anger or humiliate you in that way.

ARCHBISHOP. Keep your apologies. Save them for your trial.

JUANA. I wish only that you be aware of certain facts. Of what I did and did not intend.

ARCHBISHOP. Because you will stand trial. The Inquisition is satisfied. We have our case against you.

JUANA. I am not afraid of standing trial. I will listen to your case, whatever it might be, and I will then refute it.

ARCHBISHOP. Oh, I know how you perceive this trial; your chance to issue from the darkness of your cage and shine for all the world to see. To hold forth on a platform, with all the power and glory of an angel and watch as your detractors fall, converted to their knees. I am not entirely ignorant, you see, of such well-worn theatrics.

JUANA. I would defend my right to think and speak as I see fit.

ARCHBISHOP. But that is not how it will be. Your trial will take place quietly, with no one there to hear you speak but your inquisitors. There'll be no Father Antonio to intimate encouragement, but men who come from far away and do not know your history. Men who care not if you live or die. They will decide what to record, and what is lost upon the air. They will examine you, test you, physically and spiritually, and when they're done you will not dare to lift your head, let alone spew forth your pitiful excuses.

I am prepared to offer you redemption. If you publicly renounce the life which you have followed, the reading of all books, save for perscribed instructive texts, if you denounce the need for any nun to write in any way or form, if you renew your vows to Christ, burn those books in your possession, confess and dedicate your life upon this Earth to prayer and simple acts of charity, then I will see the charges made against you set aside, and you will be forgiven.

You have one day to think on it.

JUANA. I will not renounce my life. I know you have condemned me for writing plays and poems for the Court, but I do not regret them. For they are tales of love, of care, of despair and of devotion too; all the things which make us what we are. And there are prelates came before you, and will come after you, I think, who see no harm in them at all.

Nor can I regret the thoughts which I expressed upon your sermon. For are not all opinions put forth to be considered and responded to? Is that not the key to our progression? And why should men reserve all right to speak and write theology? If my thoughts are as learned, as exacting as a man's, why should they not be heard? And I have heard and read some poor and crude theology from men and yet it's given credence. If my arguments are flawed, if I am not as well informed as I should be, then criticise me, yes. And I will go away and think again and learn some more, and try again to reach towards the truth. Why should our faith fear knowledge? For knowledge comes from Him. And without it we would be as animals, wading through the mud and slime. Why should that light of knowledge be less precious, less miraculous in my mind than in yours? Where in the Bible does it say that girls cannot be wise? Show me, prove to me beyond all doubt that fact, and I will then be silent.

ARCHBISHOP. Here is the voice of Satan. I shudder now to hear you speak.

JUANA. There is no Devil in me. Nor do I do the Devil's work. You call on devils, I suppose, for want of any answer.

Why do you not look at me?

ARCHBISHOP. Because you are awash with sin, and I would be immune from your contagion.

JUANA. I think you are afraid of me. Of all my sex. Why? Because we cannot be controlled? Or perhaps it is yourself you fear. Because to look on woman is to know you are a man. A human being. With all the frailty that implies. And all those hours you spend at night denying your humanity, they melt away. And you are left exposed!

The ARCHBISHOP *suddenly stands and turns to face her, in a swift movement of rage. He stares at her, and she at him.*

ARCHBISHOP. You know nothing of my soul.

JUANA. Power. That's what you prize above all else. You use it as your shield.

ARCHBISHOP. I prize God's power. God's power on Earth. I have no will but His.

JUANA. You say that I abuse my faith, but I say it is you who do so.

ARCHBISHOP. You condemn yourself with every word you utter.

JUANA. Faith should not be used to subjugate, nor to degrade. Faith should not enslave our minds, but open them. It is… a flight. An expansion. An endless universe of light.

I am condemned. Yes. That I know. But you cannot reach my sense of God. You cannot reach my faith.

Silence.

ARCHBISHOP. You are the worst of devils, Sister Juana de la Cruz. The sort who whispers in our ears, 'You are all God, and born of Him, and if you have this thought then it was planted by the Lord and must therefore be right.'

JUANA. That is not what I believe. I never cease to question.

ARCHBISHOP. 'God loves you, He knows you and anything you chose to do can easily be justified because God made you, and He allows your thoughts and your desires. And if you want it, take it then – fulfill yourself. Follow your heart, for God is in your heart.' Behold your milky cult of understanding.

But you forget that we are born of sin. And Christ was born to save us from ourselves. God is not your friend. God does not dwell within you. God is the Father. The Father, Sister Juana. And if we follow your instruction, the Devil's instruction, we will cease to hear His voice and we will make a world where there is naught but selfishness and greed, debauchery, adultery, desolation. For whilst you in your cleverness can choose which stone to pull out from the edifice of God's great citadel, the people, the people will only see the cracks you leave and they will tear it down. And whilst you might endeavour to discover some personal and convoluted path to Heaven, you will leave behind you thousands by the wayside, thousands, like your niece, who make to follow you, then find themselves alone and lost upon the track. We do not want to hear your thoughts. Your thoughts are our damnation.

JUANA. My niece? Why did you say my niece?

What did you mean by that?

ARCHBISHOP. Where is your niece, Sister Juana?

JUANA. Why?

She is in her room.

ARCHBISHOP. She was pulled from the waters by the palace gates. Alive, they say, but raving. She has been taken to the asylum. There she will be delivered of the bastard child she carries.

JUANA. My niece Angelica? No. You are mistaken.

Juanita! Juanita!

JUANITA *enters*.

JUANITA. Yes, mistress?

JUANA. Find Angelica. Send her to me, please. At once.

JUANITA. Yes, mistress.

JUANITA *leaves*.

ARCHBISHOP. It was a sacred aspect of your duty – to take this innocent, your brother's child, into your care and school her in the ways of God. One you could have easily performed. But no. You smiled upon her dissipation, encouraged her transgressions, and whilst you occupied your time in courting approbation and collecting compliments, you let your charge be eaten up by sin.

JUANA. I did no such thing.

ARCHBISHOP. Oh, but you did.

JUANITA *enters*.

JUANITA. I can't find her, mistress.

JUANA. Yes, you can. Look again. Look again. Sound an alarm. Tell everyone. She must be found.

JUANITA *leaves*.

Oh, God! Oh, God! Is it true? Tell me!

ARCHBISHOP. God is angry, Sister Juana. Do you not hear His anger in the sky? And you are more the cause of it than anyone. And He will rain his anger down upon you and your kind. And all the famine, all the sickness, all the pestilence this land is yet to suffer, will be your punishment.

JUANA. Is it true?

ARCHBISHOP. You know it is.

One day, Sister Juana.

The ARCHBISHOP *leaves*.

SISTER JUANA *falls to her knees. Outside, the sky grows strangely dark, as the moon covers the sun.*

ACT FIVE

Scene One

The sound of pouring rain can be heard. In the locutory.
FATHER ANTONIO *enters, and sits down wearily. Deep in thought, he covers his face with his hands.*

MOTHER MARGUERITA *enters, and approaches him.*

FATHER ANTONIO. Mother.

MOTHER MARGUERITA. Is it done?

FATHER ANTONIO. It is done. At last. Her confession is complete. I have left her with it. To read it. To decide if she will sign.

MOTHER MARGUERITA. Surely she will? She has no choice.

FATHER ANTONIO. I have been exacting, but I feel I have been fair. I have examined separately each of her works, each of her thoughts, each of her liaisons, each failing in her duty. I have not condemned them out of hand.

MOTHER MARGUERITA. She is fortunate that you were willing to return to her.

FATHER ANTONIO. Is she? I have been thinking... I wonder if I have not failed her. I should have been firmer from the start. It should not have come to this.

MOTHER MARGUERITA. But she has always been so wilful.

FATHER ANTONIO. To see her now, so broken. I find it... She mortifies her flesh. Every morning. Every night. Her wounds are... I have asked her to desist. I think it is excessive.

MOTHER MARGUERITA. She is excessive in all things.

FATHER ANTONIO. She does not heed me. It is the wounds upon her face which...

He turns away suddenly, overcome with emotion.

MOTHER MARGUERITA. I will see to it that her wounds are properly dressed and cleaned.

FATHER ANTONIO. Juanita does her best, of course.

Forgive me, Mother. I am tired.

MOTHER MARGUERITA. These are desperate days. For all of us. Your Reverence, I should tell you, we have the sickness in the convent. I suppose it was inevitable. People have come here from the streets. Five of the sisters were taken ill last night. One of them is close to death, I fear.

FATHER ANTONIO. Plague.

MOTHER MARGUERITA. I fear so. Tonight we will make a solemn procession about the cloister. We will beg for mercy and forgiveness, upon our very knees.

FATHER ANTONIO. He was right. Aguiar y Seijas. He was right.

MOTHER MARGUERITA. Yes.

FATHER ANTONIO. God sent him here to oversee our punishment. I cannot doubt that now. He is the only certainty in all of this.

MOTHER MARGUERITA. Then we must cleave to him.

FATHER ANTONIO. He ordered that three Indians be hanged last night. On a platform in the square. For rioting. The crowd seemed ready to revolt, but he stood firm and spoke to them. And he ordered that the image of Our Lady be brought from the cathedral, for all to gaze upon. And they were silenced and dispersed.

MOTHER MARGUERITA. The Lord is present in His strength.

FATHER ANTONIO. The new-appointed Viceroy has arrived in Veracruz, they say, but he won't come near the city until the danger's passed. There is only the Church. The people know that now.

MOTHER MARGUERITA. Will it be enough for him, Father? Her confession?

FATHER ANTONIO. I believe it will be. And she wishes to renew her vows. As soon as possible.

MOTHER MARGUERITA. I will make preparations.

FATHER ANTONIO. Please do so.

I must return to her.

MOTHER MARGUERITA. Yes.

FATHER ANTONIO. Thank you, Mother.

She kisses his sleeve. He leaves.

Scene Two

SISTER JUANA*'s cell.* SISTER JUANA *has the confession in her hand.* FATHER ANTONIO *enters and waits for her to speak.*

JUANA. Who will see this?

FATHER ANTONIO. I cannot say. In normal cases, only the Archbishop; others of his prelates.

JUANA. Maria... The Vicereine... I did not think our friendship wrong. You seem to imply it was political on my part, self-serving. It was not.

FATHER ANTONIO. We talked about this. I thought you had understood.

JUANA. I do not like to see it written down. That I regret it. That I renounce it.

FATHER ANTONIO. We talked of this. It was distracting. Intense. It threatened your relationship with Christ. All your thoughts should be of Him. Of your true husband. Do you understand? I have to know you understand.

JUANA *nods.*

Will you sign?

JUANA. Yes.

FATHER ANTONIO goes to the desk.

I cannot touch a pen. I have sworn I will not.

FATHER ANTONIO. You may sign your name, I think. Tell me what else you wish to say, and I will write it for you.

She hands him the confession. He takes a pen and writes as she dictates.

JUANA. This is my full confession. I beg the Lord's forgiveness, for these my many sins. I dedicate myself to Christ, my beloved husband. I, worst of all the world...

FATHER ANTONIO. And now your name.

JUANA. I will sign in blood.

FATHER ANTONIO (*reluctantly*). Very well.

He goes to the desk and finds a fresh quill. She takes a small knife from her pocket, and cuts her arm.

No! No. Too much!

She uses the blood to fill the pen. She signs her name. FATHER ANTONIO uses a handkerchief to wrap around her arm and stem the flow of blood.

It is too much, child. You will hurt yourself irreparably. What use then would you be to God? Think of that, if nothing else. Keep this tied. Tightly.

A PRIEST enters. FATHER ANTONIO goes to him and they whisper together. He returns to SISTER JUANA.

They have come for your books.

SISTER JUANA is silent for some moments.

JUANA. They must take them, then.

FATHER ANTONIO nods to the PRIEST, who is joined by another PRIEST. They collect the books together and begin to carry them out. FATHER ANTONIO picks up three books, and puts them on SISTER JUANA's desk.

FATHER ANTONIO. You may keep this one, and your book of devotions. And your Bible.

JUANA. What will they do with them? Will they be burned?

FATHER ANTONIO. Yes. In the square.

JUANA. An Auto da Fé.

FATHER ANTONIO. Sister Juana, there are others, I think. The ones which you keep shut away.

She unlocks a drawer in her desk and opens it. She stands aside. The PRIESTS *take the books.*

JUANA. And take my jewels. These and these. Take this.

She picks up the necklace given to her by the VICEREINE.

Give them to Aguiar y Seijas. Ask him to sell them. For the poor.

FATHER ANTONIO. The Lord be praised.

The PRIESTS *finish their work and leave.* SISTER JUANA *looks about her, at the near-empty cell.*

FATHER ANTONIO *takes up her confession.*

I will take your confession to the Archbishop. Immediately. And I will tell him of the great, the wondrous progress you have made. I will tell him that you would renew your vows.

JUANA. Let it be soon.

FATHER ANTONIO. You will find peace, Sister Juana. That is my promise to you. If I do nothing else before I die...

He starts to go.

JUANA. Father? How is she? Do you know?

FATHER ANTONIO. She is alive. I know no more than that.

JUANA. Will you go to her? For me? Tell her that I love her. Ask her to forgive me. Though it cannot be forgiven. Tell her that I love her.

FATHER ANTONIO. I will then.

JUANA. Thank you.

FATHER ANTONIO. May the Lord bless you and keep you. (*Blessing her.*) In the name of the Father, the Son, and the Holy Spirit. Amen.

JUANA. Amen.

He leaves. SISTER JUANA *sinks to her knees.*

Angelica.

She cries for a moment, then recovers herself. JUANITA *enters and looks about at the empty room.*

JUANITA. They took everything. Why did they take everything?

(*Seeing* SISTER JUANA*'s arm.*) But what have you done there?

She goes to SISTER JUANA *and kneels beside her. She examines her arm.*

JUANA. It doesn't matter.

Tears spring to JUANITA*'s eyes.*

JUANITA. Mistress… I cannot bear to see you so.

JUANA. She tried to talk to me. She asked me about Hell. I told her to be quiet.

JUANITA. Mistress, please. You know the fault was all with me. And I cannot forgive myself. And if I ever do find out who let her pass beyond the garden, I'll…

JUANA. The fault was mine. She was not in your charge.

JUANITA. But…

JUANA. The fault was mine. And there will be no more crying. Why should we have that luxury? She cannot cry her life back.

JUANITA. Poor child.

JUANA. I think there is no end to my self-pity. I realised today, for all these weeks of my confession, I have been asking God why He created me this way; why He cursed me with this mind, when really… it is me. It's me. Free will. I always preached free will. The gift was His, but it was I, and I alone, who chose how I would use it. And I chose to make of it a gross, and a malignant thing.

JUANITA. No.

JUANA. Oh yes.

JUANITA. Look here, my mistress –

She takes a book from her pocket.

This came for you. From Spain. It arrived a week ago, but Mother Marguerita said you mustn't see it, until you'd finished your confession. It's from the Vicereine. A volume of your poems. And look, here at the front, there are some letters from important priests, who say your work is wonderful, and they are full of praise for you.

Look. Look how gorgeously it's bound. Take it.

JUANA. No. I do not want to hear of it again. Or see it. You keep it if you wish to.

JUANITA. But...

JUANA. I want only to be left alone with God. To ask forgiveness, endlessly. To love Him and to pray that He will love me in return. That's all.

Pause.

I am not sad, Juanita. For in the very heart of me I always longed to clear away the world and find my way to Him. To lose myself. This burden.

Pause.

JUANITA. I will keep it for you then.

And read it too, from time to time.

It was you who taught me how to read. I remember when they used to say, 'Better that the slaves don't read. Let their minds live in the dark.' But you sat down with me. And with my finger traced the letters, one by one. And that was right.

I believe in you, Sister Juana. Just as you believe in me.

JUANITA *goes to stand, but* SISTER JUANA *reaches out to her and hugs her, holds her closely.* JUANITA *kisses her head.*

JUANA (*quietly*). Keep it.

JUANITA *nods her head. She stands.*

JUANITA. I'll fetch some water for your arm. Then I'll prepare your bed for you.

A wailing and a crying is heard, as the NUNS *begin to process around the cloister.*

JUANA. What's that? What's happening? Is that my sisters?

JUANITA. Yes. They are processing round the cloister. I saw them lift the wooden crosses from the walls.

JUANA. Why? Because of me? To atone for me?

JUANITA. No, mistress.

JUANA. Then what? Tell me.

JUANITA. The sickness is in the convent.

JUANA. What sickness?

JUANITA. The worst.

JUANA. How many?

JUANITA. Five. Sister Sebastiana is very ill.

JUANA. I must go to them. I must join them. If they will allow me to.

JUANITA. You can't. You're far too weak.

JUANA. I'm not.

JUANITA. Look at you. You can't. They will not cease till dawn.

JUANA. Nor will I. I have to go to them.

JUANITA. Then I shall never leave your side.

They leave.

Scene Three

In the locutory. The bell to the gate rings repeatedly. After a few moments, BISHOP SANTA CRUZ *enters. He is carrying a basket of bread and fruit in one hand. He places it down. He takes out a handkerchief and covers his nose.*

SANTA CRUZ. Hello?

After a few moments, BRIGIDA *enters, from the cloister.*

BRIGIDA. Oh, it's you, my lord.

SANTA CRUZ. I rang but no one came. The gate was not locked.

BRIGIDA. It wouldn't be.

SANTA CRUZ (*pointing to the basket*). That had been left outside.

BRIGIDA. Thank you. People have been very kind. And when there is so little to go round.

SANTA CRUZ. I was sorry to hear about Sister Sebastiana.

BRIGIDA. Yes. She's in a better place now. She was too good for this world. I always said so.

SANTA CRUZ. Yes.

BRIGIDA. Mother Marguerita is unwell. I doubt that she'll receive you.

SANTA CRUZ. It's Sister Juana I have come to see.

BRIGIDA. Sister Juana?

JUANITA enters from the cloister. She is clutching a piece of paper in her hand.

SANTA CRUZ. Ah, Juanita. I wish to speak with your mistress. She will need a new confessor. For Father Antonio is dead. He caught a cold, and with his age, the sickness took him quickly.

JUANITA. They went together then.

SANTA CRUZ. Together?

JUANITA. Sister Juana is dead.

> SANTA CRUZ *is stunned. Silent.*

> She died last night. She had spent every hour of late nursing her sisters. She cared nothing for herself. And she was weak. And full of grief.

SANTA CRUZ. Sister Juana is dead.

> May I see her?

JUANITA. No. I know she would not want that.

SANTA CRUZ. Did she leave anything? Any letters? Any words?

JUANITA (*holding up the paper in her hand*). Only this. She took up her pen, and wrote for me my freedom.

> JUANITA *stands very still. Tears fall down her face.* BRIGIDA *takes up the basket.*

BRIGIDA. Come, Juanita. Let's go and make some use of these good things. And nurse the sisters tenderly, until this dreadful time is passed. For we can do no more.

> *They leave.* SANTA CRUZ *is left alone.*

SANTA CRUZ. Dead then. This feels like a calamity. Yet why should I perceive it to be so? She mattered not to me. Though, truth be told, I was rather relishing, I think, the thought of coming here today; of lifting her, a bird with broken wings, from off the floor, and recreating her in my own image. But there. She has eluded me.

> Sleep well, Sister Juana.

> When I become Archbishop, as I am sure to do in time, I'll find some means to honour her. A stone in the cathedral perhaps. Nowhere too prominent. A simple mention of her name. For she was remarkable, in her own way.

The End.

A Nick Hern Book

The Heresy of Love first published in Great Britain as a paperback original in 2012 by Nick Hern Books Limited, The Glasshouse, 49a Goldhawk Road, London W12 8QP, in association with the Royal Shakespeare Company

Reprinted 2014

The Heresy of Love copyright © 2012 Helen Edmundson

Cover illustration by Emmanuel Polanco
Cover design by Ned Hoste, 2H

Typeset by Nick Hern Books, London
Printed in the UK by Mimeo Ltd, Huntingdon, Cambridgeshire PE29 6XX

A CIP catalogue record for this book is available from the British Library

ISBN 978 1 84842 239 1

CAUTION All rights whatsoever in this play are strictly reserved. Requests to reproduce the text in whole or in part should be addressed to the publisher.

Amateur Performing Rights Applications for performance, including readings and excerpts, by amateurs in the English language throughout the world (excluding the USA and Canada) should be made before rehearsals begin to the Performing Rights Manager, Nick Hern Books, The Glasshouse, 49a Goldhawk Road, London W12 8QP, *tel* +44 (0)20 8749 4953, *e-mail* info@nickhernbooks.co.uk, except as follows:

Australia: Dominie Drama, 8 Cross Street, Brookvale 2100, *fax* (2) 9938 8695, *e-mail* drama@dominie.com.au

New Zealand: Play Bureau, PO Box 9013, St Clair, Dunedin 9047, *tel* (3) 455 9959, *e-mail* play.bureau.nz@xtra.co.nz

South Africa: DALRO (pty) Ltd, PO Box 31627, 2017 Braamfontein, *tel* (11) 712 8000, *fax* (11) 403 9094, *e-mail* theatricals@dalro.co.za

United States of America and Canada: The Agency (London) Ltd, see details below

Professional Performing Rights Application for performance by professionals in any medium and in any language throughout the world (and amateur and stock performances in the United States of America and Canada) should be addressed to The Agency (London) Ltd, 24 Pottery Lane, Holland Park, London W11 4LZ, *fax* +44 (0)20 7727 9037, *e-mail* info@theagency.co.uk

No performance of any kind may be given unless a licence has been obtained. Applications should be made before rehearsals begin. Publication of this play does not necessarily indicate its availability for amateur performance.

MIX
Paper from
responsible sources
FSC® C019549